The Astonishing

DREAM

of

JOB

Ernie L. Vecchio

Copyright © 2012 Ernie L. Vecchio

All rights reserved.

ISBN:0985469501

ISBN-13:9780985469504

Edited by Brooke Warner
www.warnercoaching.com

Cover Photo by Justin Lowery
Web, Graphic & New Media Designer
http://www.justinlowery.com

Table of Contents

Preface i

Fate 1

The Comparison 25

Voices 43

The Tirade 75

I Will Ask 93

The Companion 113

Humbled by the Ego 129

The Human Spark 149

Kept in the Dark 169

The Answer to Why 183

Epilogue 211

About the Author 217

ζ

Preface

Book of JOB Synopsis

There was an extremely pious man named Job. He was very prosperous, and had seven sons and three daughters. Constantly fearing that his sons may have sinned and "cursed God in their hearts," he habitually offered burnt offerings as a pardon for their sins.

A divine council of angels and the accuser or adversary (Satan) presented themselves to God. God asked Satan his opinion on Job, apparently a truly pious man. Satan answered that Job was pious only because he was prosperous. In response to Satan's assertion, God gave Satan permission to destroy Job's possessions and family.

All of Job's possessions were destroyed and the wind caused the house of his firstborn to collapse, killing all of Job's offspring who were gathered for a feast. Job did not curse God after this but instead shaved his head, tore off his clothes, and said, "Naked I came out of my mother's womb, and naked shall I return: Lord has given, and Lord has taken away; blessed be the name of Lord."

Job endured these first calamities without reproach. Meanwhile, Satan solicited permission to afflict his person as well, and God said, "Behold, he is in your hand, but don't touch his life." Satan, therefore, smote him with dreadful boils, and Job, seated in ashes, scraped his skin with broken pottery. His wife prompted him to "curse God, and die", but Job answered, "You speak as one of the foolish speaks. Moreover, shall we receive good from God and shall not receive evil?"

Hearing of the evil that has befallen Job, three of his friends came to console him. There was a fourth who played a significant role in the dialogue; however, his arrival was not described. His friends spent seven days sitting on the ground with Job, without saying anything to him because they saw that he was suffering and in much pain. Finally, Job broke his silence and "curses the day he was born."

In the epilogue, God condemned Job's friends for their ignorance and lack of understanding while commending Job for his righteous words. He then commanded them to prepare burnt offerings and reassured them that Job will pray for their forgiveness. Job was restored to health, gaining double the riches he possessed before and having seven sons and three daughters (his wife did not die in this ordeal). His new daughters were the most beautiful in the land, and each was given inheritance along with their brothers. Job was blessed once again and lived on for another 140 year's living to see his children to the fourth generation and dying peacefully of old age.

1

Fate

The mountains of West Virginia are beautiful in the fall. The leaves are just starting to change color and the temperatures are always refreshing after a hot summer. As I drove out to the lodge where I was meeting Pieta for dinner, I noticed that the leaves still glistened from a recent rain and the air held a damp green smell of renewal. The early evening sun cast a perfect light deepening the colors.

It was no coincidence that Pieta chose the old lodge as our meeting place. We'd held several retreats there and loved the surrounding parks. When I arrived, I parked my truck and searched the back seat for my cell phone. Pieta, I suspected, would already be in the restaurant, waiting patiently. We'd spoken on the phone a year ago, but this call was different. He was more excited than usual and eager to share something with me.

I got out of my car and slowly approached the rustic log-structured lodge with its large deck and winding steps. In the distance, I could hear the sounds of nature, birds chirping and waterfalls crashing. Glancing at my watch, it was just past 6:00 p.m. I was a few minutes late.

The Astonishing Dream of JOB

As I approached the restaurant, memories of my friendship with Pieta flooded my thoughts. He'd always been a deeply spiritual man, and the closer I got to the lodge, the more eager I felt to hear about this profound message he had mentioned on the phone—a thirty-six hundred-year-old dream written down but never interpreted.

"You'll see," he'd said, his words tumbling on top of each other. "This dream is going to blow your mind! It answers so many profound questions about the human experience."

"Can we meet to talk about it? The message in this ancient dream supports your teachings—you will love it."

Supports my teachings? I had met Pieta as I was entering the psychology field. Amazingly, that was almost forty years ago now. Green and naïve about the profession, he nurtured me along one question at a time. I was privy to his own development, too, particularly as he evolved spiritually. I was an agnostic who began with a Presbyterian orientation and he was a Mormon with deep spiritual roots. He came from a stable family that had survived the Great Depression. Mine was alcoholic and abusive, throwing me out with the bath water. Each of us worked in environments where human suffering dominated our clinical experience: a trauma hospital. Supportive of my teachings? The only thing I could come up with on the drive over was that he was referring to what I'd come to learn about the culture's definition of compassion.

The country lodge was more crowded than I thought it would be for a Sunday. Maybe it was the church crowd from the surrounding small community, I thought. As I wove my way into the dining room, Pieta waved at me from the corner. He was sitting by a window that overlooked the waterfalls.

I noticed a commotion at the table next to him. People were shuffling and cooing and the manager had come over

Fate

to break up the noise. When everyone dispersed, I could see what was getting so much attention: a puppy, in a basket under the table. Pieta leaned over to scratch it behind the ears and gave me a smile as I approached. "You've got to love puppies! They are the ultimate magnet," he said.

He loosened his jacket to make himself comfortable and stood up to shake my hand. "Lou," he said. "You look fantastic! How are you?" Taking his hand, I pulled him toward me in a hug. Pieta was usually not this physical. But, I wanted him to know how much I missed him. I'd forgotten how dark he could get when he'd been in the sun. I noticed he was a little grayer around the edges, but the calm that emanated from his face soothed me. This I remembered well.

***

"Thank you for coming on such short notice," Pieta said. I could tell the hug had made him a little uncomfortable.

"Well, I could hardly ignore your request. I don't remember you ever sounding so excited by something."

"Yes, it's true," Pieta smiled. "Sit down. I have much to tell you."

I removed my coat and sat in the corner closest to the scenic view. We ordered coffee and spent the first thirty minutes telling old stories and remembering our first meeting. I was always comfortable sharing the newest transitions in my own spiritual process with him. Pieta seemed to understand what I was experiencing and would usually expand on my revelations.

"So are you still embracing change like I remember?" he asked.

I had always had difficulty hiding my feelings from Pieta. He was one of my few friends who actually knew me. Though it had only been a year since we'd last spoken—and longer than that since we'd seen each other—it felt like we had barely been apart. "I've missed your gift of being able to see me. Do you want the truth?"

"Is there anything else?" he asked.

"Well, the truth is, I am changing so much internally these days that very little of what I thought was real about my life remains. I've been considering moving someplace more remote, somewhere that supports my passion for teaching."

"I remember that you said there were a couple more books in you. Is that part of the plan as well?"

"It is," I said. "But I still struggle with whether anybody cares about what I think and feel about the cultural distortion I've discovered."

"You mean how we've come to define compassion as a culture, right?" he asked.

"Yes," I said. "I'm not sure if anybody really cares."

He smiled. "So what are you going to do?"

"I'm still sorting it out," I said. "I just know that I am moving internally and I don't want to get in my own way."

Typical of Pieta, he inverted my concerns by remarking, "Sounds as if you are entering the wonderful place of uncertainty."

"Uh, I guess," I said. "Can we order some coffee? Are you hungry?" I asked.

"Sure," he answered, beckoning the waitress. "Well, I can tell you this: Your struggle is in this thirty-six-hundred-year-old dream."

The restaurant fell away to white. He had my full attention. Not even the puppy in the basket distracted me. "Tell me more about this dream," I said.

Fate

He looked out the window, then back at me. "I told you on the phone that I was researching the location of Job's experience in the Bible. I found out it specifically took place in Iraq. An interesting coincidence since we went to war there searching for weapons of mass destruction—and there weren't any. The more I looked into this, the more exciting it became. A translation of an ancient Sumerian text, the Erra Epos, relates a story of catastrophic destruction, on a scale comparable to nuclear weapons, about the same time in history as The Book of Job—at the Sinai Peninsula in the city of Sodom and Gomorrah. This would have created some sort of nuclear cloud that would have been carried by the prevailing winds eastward, causing death and desolation to anything in its path. So it seems there were weapons of mass destruction in Iraq after all, just thirty-six hundred years ago."

Our coffee and dinner arrived, but we were so absorbed in conversation we barely noticed.

"And what does this mean in the context of Job's experience?" I asked.

"Well," he said, "as you know, I've been working to finish my Doctorate in Divinity this year, but none of my teachers seems to know the author of The Book of Job. Nor are any of them sure when it was written. All they know is that it predates Christ by at least a thousand years. And when I wanted to explore its origins more deeply, they didn't want to discuss it with me."

"That's interesting," I said, "though I can understand church educators being protective of their turf."

"Yes, but the more questions I asked, the more disturbed the church faculty became. The biblical teaching of this story has always been about Job's faith or patience—that he is rewarded in the end for his loyalty to God. And it addresses the age-old question of why righteous people suffer."

"Or why any of us suffer for that matter," I replied.

"Job is described in the Bible as a man of Uz. The location of Uz is uncertain. Biblical scholars suspect that it was near Edom, south/southeast of the Dead Sea. Others believe it was located far north of Palestine, near Haran, the home territory of Abraham. But now it turns out that Sodom and Gomorrah were destroyed in Job's time by brimstone and fire and many scholars believe it's beneath the waters of the Dead Sea."

"And why is this significant?" I asked.

"Because, what if Job was in the path of that destruction? What if the winds carried the fallout to his location?"

"Yes, I'm following," I said.

"This would support Job having had a natural experience that he interpreted as God. What if what's always been interpreted as an external struggle with God was actually an internal struggle with what was happening to him as the result of this severe storm?"

"That would be an amazing way to look at the text," I said.

Pieta paused and looked at me with an uncharacteristic smirk. "Bear with me," he finally said. "Did you know that God was a gambler?"

"What?" I laughed. "Imagine, we have been taught that there was a historical moment when two deities, God and Satan, had a bet!" he said, smiling.

"I must admit," I said. "That does sound a little ridiculous. This is the problem with interpreting the Bible as the literalists do—like historical fact. And besides, there is no way we could truly know this, let alone record it."

"I agree." he said. "The way the story goes, Satan bets God that Job, though righteous, has a weakness. He accuses

God of protecting Job and his wealth from any kind of harm. Said differently, Satan is betting that Job serves God only because of his material possessions. Thus, he challenges God to take them away."

"Oh, I see. Gambling deities," I said, pondering the implication of what he was saying.

"Yes," he replied smiling. "And God takes the bet, as long as Satan doesn't attack Job physically."

"I had actually forgotten that portion of the story," I said. "I'm interested in where you are going with this."

"It gets better. Keep in mind that Job is unaware that his life is being played with like this. Oh, he does stay devoted to God, but guess what happens next?"

"What?" I asked.

"Satan argues that since Job's health was preserved, he has not really been tested. And, if God would allow such a test, Job would certainly curse God then."

"So, Satan raises the stakes?" I replied.

"Yes," he said. "And, God takes the bet as long as Job isn't killed."

"Okay," I laughed. "So God is a gambler. Pieta, I appreciate you helping me re-member these facts about the story, but what does this have to do with our meeting tonight?" I asked.

"Well," he said. "I met a spiritual teacher who heard about me questioning the significance of the Book of Job. I need to keep his name anonymous, but he's agreed to let me bounce my ideas off him. He confirmed that an ancient writing describing Job's experience as a dream has been recently discovered! Also, that the messages it revealed are profound and fitting of modern times."

Pieta paused for a moment, as if waiting for some reaction, but the reasons for his excitement still eluded me. I didn't know what to say.

"My teacher said that the timeline of Job's experience is still a subject of great debate. It was before Moses, or 1500 B.C., at the time of Solomon 900 B.C., and possibly as late as 600 B.C. The best we can say is that it appears the Book of Job was written near the end of the Old Testament period, but we cannot be more precise than that. To my knowledge, no one has carbon dated the age of the dream document yet."

Pieta took a sip of coffee, set his cup back on the table, and continued. "Okay, so here goes. This new document reveals that Job is actually speaking to his ego from the heart. When he is left in despair as a result of this severe storm, and seemingly losing everything, he is asking: "Why?" Not, why is the storm happening to him, as the Bible interpreters suggest, but rather why he is so afraid. He is speaking to his fear. "Why should I listen to you, fear, when my heart has never lied to me?" His question is suggesting that when the heart is convinced of truth we should not doubt it, no matter how frightened or lost we feel. Imagine, the Book of Job may represent the birth of recorded feelings. Remember, feelings are different than emotions. Feelings are a reaction to the present moment, and the organ of perception is the heart. Emotions are a re-enactment of a previous experience, tied to memories that involve the brain. The recent discovery of Job's experience as a dream has the potential to bring us a lost message about feelings."

"Now I understand," I said.

Pieta nodded. "You can see then, with all the buzz of spiritual transformation happening today, this is perfect timing," he said.

Fate

"Yes, yes I can," I answered, feeling the energy of Pieta's excitement coursing through me.

"Finally!" he said almost knocking over his coffee. "We've got something here that could add some depth to the spiritual movement across the planet. It has the possibility of impacting millions of people. The spiritual transformation everyone is speaking of has a missing piece. It seems that we've mistaken being more conscientious or 'present' as the transformation, when; in fact, these are necessary layers of awareness. We are still missing what humans need, to move to the next level. The discovery of this ancient dream actually gives us a renewed respect for the intelligence of the heart. Job's desire thirty-six hundred years ago was to trust his heart's perspective about what was happening to him. He was convinced that his heart knew the truth."

"What truth?" I asked.

Pieta's eyes unexpectedly filled with tears. "My spiritual teacher told me that the answer to that question enters awareness when you begin to realize what Job was experiencing internally—that our heart's intelligence is greater than the ego. This is spiritually profound, even in contemporary times. The dream is offering us an opportunity to view the conversation in this biblical story as a deep experience of self-talk from someone in the throes of despair. Each layer of suffering offers truths about the mind, body, spirit relationship. Job is having an internal experience brought on by a natural event—a storm. Whoever wrote the dream text, in fact, is pleading for his internal experience to be interpreted and shared with the world. This is not what the bible interpreters did. According to the dream text, Job's experience was intended to teach us that there is an ethical way to suffer and the heart knows how. This is precisely what Oswald Chambers[1] said in the 1890s.

Pieta was correct. This new find was supportive of my teachings about trauma. Job's decision to listen to his heart in his lowest possible moment was an accurate feeling of compassion or self-love. An essential step in the healing process, but also important for spiritual transformation. It was all clicking into place now. Pieta was trying to tell me that "suffering with" himself brought about growth, while "suffering for" himself would have left him broken. This was affirmed in my own work with trauma. Somehow, Job knew this.

"Do you think people will accept this?" I asked.

Before Pieta could even answer, though, I interrupted to clarify my concerns.

"Have you seen the news lately," I asked. "Do we look like a society that wants to learn something new about suffering? Most of us are convinced we are all destined to be victims, don't you think?"

My interest in the soul's intent as the organizing intelligence that guides a human life had consumed my career. I knew that many of my clients over the years had spun their victim stories with little or no personal growth. I was beginning to believe that only a few chosen people could actually grow from their suffering. I'd seen many trauma patients awaken during their recovery but only a few stayed awake.

Just as I said this, the television at the lodge bar flashed a CNN breaking news re-port about an earthquake in Chile. From where I sat I could read the scrolling information below the talking head: "Death toll in Chile reaches 708 after an 8.8 magnitude earthquake hits the country. Local police are battling looters and using tear gas for crowd control." Every head in the lodge turned toward the screen in that moment, captivated by the scenes of rubble and shock.

A man got up from a table nearby, causing a woman seated at another table to yell, "Would you get out of the damn way! Some of us want to see what is going on! Are you deaf? Jesus Christ!" The woman took a drink of her coffee and appeared quite proud of her public display.

The poor little puppy at the table next to ours shocked by the volume of the woman's voice, jumped from his basket and ran toward the door. Its owner ran after it, shouting angrily, "Thanks a lot, lady!"

Pieta and I both stared for a long while. It was unclear which was more distracting—news of the earthquake or the drama that was unfolding in the restaurant around us. Finally Pieta looked away from the tragedy on the screen and said, "It seems we don't get to choose if we suffer, but because of this new understanding of Job's experience we can choose how."

"What will that mean for people today?"

"Consciousness will rise with the realization that the heart's intelligence is above the ego," he said. "And, according to my spiritual teacher, the connection to our heart was initially forced out of our awareness by a deep feeling of injustice."

"Injustice," I asked. "You mean a collective feeling that something was done to us?"

"Yes, and that's the rub!" he replied. "Most of us may never figure it out. By viewing the Book of Job as a dream, however, we begin to get a glimpse of what happened—that our story is actually driven by the human spirit. The human spirit is defined as that which is—around and through—all that is. My teacher says that our ability to cultivate the higher self was stolen. We had our first experience with anger, which then attacked and left us passive and dependent. Then, we were introduced to the human shadow, which used its powers to rob our ability to handle life in general. It's a lot to take in!"

The Astonishing Dream of JOB

I understood where Pieta was going with this. He was implying that suffering happens to everyone. But, the significance of Job's experience was that if he didn't figure out how to suffer with himself, all future generations would be lost suffering for themselves as victims of the ego. As a psychologist, I saw this in people and the culture every day. Ironically, Job learned this distinction, and yet here we were, thirty-six hundred years later, just opening our eyes to the implications of his discovery.

"Do you think this injustice of losing oneself as victim is behind that woman's angry outburst?" I joked.

"Yes, we are all walking around angry and we don't know why. With this anger comes a sense of entitlement. Our anger exists because we are afraid, but we've lost the capacity to distinguish between real and imagined fear. So this lack of discrimination has become the source of our paranoia, and it's affecting everyone."

Pieta looked around the room at all the patrons watching the television. "And when it comes to suffering, we're just glad it's happening to someone else and not to us."

I knew what he said was true. In my own work with severe trauma victims, I had witnessed that few of my patients took their adversity and used it to grow spiritually. I have always been in awe of the human spirit when it comes to life challenges. Human beings are incredibly resilient if they don't "spin" into their victimization.

"Can you explain more about this injustice that we're feeling?" I asked.

"I spoke with my spiritual teacher about this," he replied, "and he said it has to do with lost potential and our inability to nourish ourselves. Losing or detaching from the heart's wisdom when initially faced with adversity leaves many of us barren, lonely, and feeling isolated and hopeless. It weakens our very foundation."

Fate

Everything Pieta said hit me personally and described many of my patients. Most of them never reached their potential because of the treatment they received from significant family members or life circumstances. When they did have opportunities, so few of them were prepared to reach out and grab them. I knew it to be true that so many people are so busy surviving our lives that we rarely go after our dreams.

"My mentor has seen the dream text," Pieta continued, "and says it suggests that when our spirit is broken early, we will find it very difficult to trust our feelings again."

"That's painful to realize as so many of us seem to have this problem," I said.

"That was my reaction as well," he replied. "But my teacher said to remember that most of the culture will never realize that the human spirit provokes our emotional suffering, and sometimes it seems without reason. In truth, moment-by-moment we emotionally sacrifice our lives to preserve our ego and its attachments. Often, this means our ego is asleep and we are swimming in our emotions. The reason for the human spirit's provocation is for us to feel our way through our lives and to let go so our ego can awaken. That is, move from a moral right or wrong existence to an ethical or true state of being. Said differently, to remember to trust our feelings rather than be at the mercy of our emotions. This new interpretation of the Book of Job could help grow our understanding around this distinction."

"Okay," I said. "Can you explain further what the heart is convinced of?"

Pieta hesitated, pulling his thoughts together.

"This is where it gets a little confusing," he said. "But my mentor put it this way. We begin as 'spirited' human beings. Our view of life is innocent, sincere, and humble. We never question our fears. At our disposal are the potential for mental perfection, healing, wholeness, and the attainment of a higher state of consciousness. Essentially, we have access to an inner ability to feel whole. Eastern philosophy would say we initially possessed the secret of a middle path—in a conflicting world of duality."

"And then what happened?" I asked.

"In ancient times, when we felt inspired by the heart's intelligence, this inspiration was controlled by an inner warning: Never forget the fear and judgment of ego. The inner struggle to BE was combined with being afraid of fear itself. These were our spiritual beginnings. Imagine—we may be able to finally let fear and judgment go!"

I was silent for a moment. "So, what you're saying is that being afraid of being afraid was the start of our spiritual journey?" I asked.

Pieta leaned toward me. "That's exactly right! Have you ever paid attention to the voices in your head? Do you have a sense of what they are? Ever wondered about their function in your daily life? Is soul and spirit clear in your mind as unique human gifts? When life takes over, do you get distracted from them, and suddenly think they disappear?"

"Well," he continued, "according to my teacher, the voices serve the ego but not necessarily the heart. Their chatter affects our every thought and creates ideas that are negative and sometimes even repulsive."

"Job's experience as an ancient dream suggests that in that moment we should ask this question: Do I humbly serve the ego's chatter and allow myself to spiritually die, or do I keep my heart in the equation?"

I knew he wanted me to say, "Go with our hearts", but I was still digesting every-thing he'd said so far. My hesitation didn't slow him down at all.

"Don't you see?" he asked. "The human spirit—that which is around and through all that is—actually provokes the ego into action. Nobody in the mental health profession speaks about the ego in this way. Instead, the culture tells us there is a right action and judges our choices. As a result, self-judgment and self-blame become the cause of our initial suffering and block our growth. Essentially, we are not conscious of the 'why' for this provocation. In truth, if the human spirit was not tenacious we would never awaken to the importance of our feelings, nor would we spiritually mature. This dream text gives us the unconscious reason why: unaware and emotionally frightened we are fated to serve the ego! Suffering with ourselves offsets this fate. Suffering for ourselves reinforces the ego's hold on us as victims. Using our heart's intelligence as a compass, we can navigate through this conditioning and serve the truth of who we are."

The excitement in Pieta's voice and his passion was intoxicating.

"You are really captivated by this, aren't you?" I asked.

"Is this not exactly what you want to teach the public about how we do compassion in our culture?" he asked.

I looked at Pieta and said, "Yes, and I can't imagine a better message than one that would teach us a healthier way to suffer what it means to be human. It is the core of all spiritual teachings, and yet so few people understand this."

Adjusting his coffee cup and taking a bite of dinner, Pieta continued, "Job's story as a dream is significant because of when it happened in history. It is a rare examination of the inner workings of a suffering and spiritual human being—a thousand years before Christ. Today, so many people are seeking integrity. Taking this approach to the Book of Job could essentially restore the integrity of the human heart!"

"What do you mean?" I asked.

The Astonishing Dream of JOB

"My teacher says that in the beginning we naturally feel our way through life and then, because of some unexpected and internalized adversity, we end up emotional about what happened. Attaching to the memory of that event, we lose ourselves to simple survival. We shift from a heartfelt existence to one of repetitive ego re-enactments. In this instance, Job was reacting to the storm and wanting to prevent his ego from attacking him. The suggestion is that he had no previous memory of being this afraid, nothing to re-enact. So, when the ego began to berate him with guilt and shame, he was temporarily lost to these emotions. Somehow, Job knew that his feelings had more integrity than his emotions. In other words, he trusted his heart. Imagine how much better we would treat ourselves and others with this kind of trust. In our culture, we've become afraid of emoting in general. This is because our emotions are tied to the grief of losing oneself—to fear. In Western culture, guilt is I made a mistake, while shame is I am a mistake. The deep wound of shaming is what Job was questioning: in his heart he feels fine. Meanwhile, his fears and emotions are telling him otherwise. This pattern is deeply ingrained in the psyche of our culture, whether people are aware of it or not."

"So, we became untrusting of our feelings and shifted from feeling beings to emotional beings?" I asked.

"Yes," he said. "Doesn't this sound like clinical depression to you? The dream describes a gloomily somber force that seizes our emotions for days and sometimes months. The text even implies that in this experience Job pondered suicide. Imagine, psychiatry makes a living because we believe our emotions are a curse!"

"That's astonishing," I said.

"My spiritual teacher says the dream manuscript reports Job as having said: 'Let a threat of self-harm occur and be made real by something large and formidable. Let natural light be darkened by my confusion and uncertainty. If life is to be this emotional, then it has to be seen as it really is—dark and difficult.'"

"Hmmm," I said. "It's almost as if Job is questioning his emotional health?"

Pieta couldn't control his energy. "There is no doubt that one thousand years be-fore Christ someone was asking why humans feel? More important, they asked why awareness comes during suffering. Is that not profound? Because of this find, feelings could be recognized again as having merit. We can make the case that they are more valid than our thoughts."

"Because most people think feelings are the same things as emotions, right?" I asked.

"Yes. Exactly!" He said. "When in truth feelings are a barometer for the quality of our thoughts. If they are contaminated by the ego's influence, they become an emotion which gives energy and motion to faulty or harmful thinking. For many, this is a vicious cycle in their heads."

"And you're worried about the church's reaction to this interpretation of a biblical text?" I asked, recalling what he'd said earlier about the reaction from his faculty.

"Personally, I'm not," he said. "But my mentor is. That is the reason he wants to remain anonymous. He is reclusive and at a place spiritually where he is uncertain about bringing controversy or negative energy to his life. Hopefully, we can influence him to come forward because he understands this discovery better than anyone."

"As for the church's reaction, I don't think interpreting Job's experience as a dream does a disservice to what theology says is the author's intent at all," he continued. "In fact, it is turning out to reveal several spiritual truths that are not available in their interpretation."

The Astonishing Dream of JOB

For several minutes we fiddled with our food and gazed out the window. The sun had begun to set and many of the restaurant's patrons were starting to leave. Finally, Pieta looked at me and asked, "So are you interested in learning more?"

"I want to remain open," I said. I have long known that we have little guidance when it comes to dealing with the disappointments of life. To think that someone who lived thirty-six hundred years ago was struggling with being human and that there may be an interpretation of an experience that could better teach us how to handle adversity is mind-blowing."

"Have you seen the dream text?" I asked.

"No, all I have are my recordings with my mentor. Each time we've spoken on the phone or I've been to his house, I've taken notes or taped our discussions."

Again we were quiet, lost in thought.

"Well," he said, "now you know why I needed to talk with you."

"Yes, this is absolutely profound stuff—if it's true," I said.

He smiled.

"What?" I asked.

"The dream says that proof happens when the heart has been convinced."

"What does that mean?"

"Trusting our feelings validates the heart's intelligence. When we truly stick with what we know is ethical to the self, we begin to become aligned with the soul's intent."

I hesitated for a second. Is there some validity in this new interpretation? Do we all secretly feel this injustice the dream speaks of? Will an awareness of the origin of fear and anger shed light on the human experience? Are we destined to suffer uselessly? Is this really our fate?

"I'm not sure how to feel about this," I said. "Certainly, the way the word spirituality is used broadly in our culture is such that it tends to mean whatever a person wants it to mean."

"Yes," he replied.

"So we're all trying to find a context that works for us?" I asked.

Now the sun had dropped fully behind the mountain, leaving a tint of red light that outlined the edge of the nearby hills. Pieta was correct. If we could find a context for what it means to be human—not defining ourselves simply by our families, culture, and adversities—then we could find out what it means to just simply be.

"I can tell you this," I said. "Though I have a working definition of spirituality, if this ancient dream can help me better understand the interior of my own experiences, I want to hear more. I think the general public will feel the same way."

Pieta stood up and insisted he pay for our dinner. Together we walked to the front of the lodge and the evening air felt wonderful on my face as we moved to a picnic shelter. It was completely dark now, and I contemplated how true spirituality, at least for me, was a quest for a fulfilled and authentic life. I knew Pieta felt the same way.

"Spirituality and the human potential movement have somehow merged today," he said.

"Yes, and it's more confusing than ever what either of these two have to do with one's relationship with God," I said.

"The beauty of the teaching that comes from this ancient dream is that, though it is rooted in scripture, it offers an experiential way to look at the message, one that may resonate with a lot of people."

"We're definitely making a shift in consciousness," he said. "Modern-day spirituality is beginning to mirror nineteenth-century American transcendentalists like Ralph Waldo Emerson and Henry David Thoreau. Wasn't it one of those guys who said: 'I should not talk so much about myself, if there were anybody else whom I knew as well'?"

"Exactly," I replied. "It was my early reading of transcendental authors like them that influenced my desire to pursue self-understanding and spiritual growth. Most of those guys were saying then that the road less traveled is the one taken inward. Conversations like the one we're having reflect how long we've been searching, doesn't it?"

"Longer than both of us would probably like to admit," he smiled. "The dream text is essentially a lesson from the Old Testament. But the message is much different than religious scholars teach. This could pose a problem for a lot of people."

I walked to the overlook where we could see the falls in the shadows. The lodge had lined the edge of the adjoining creek with green lights. Mist rose from the crashing water. It had been a long time since I'd had such a rich conversation with anyone. Pieta had a knack of taking me to a reflective place.

"What is it about nature that is so calming?" Pieta asked from behind me.

I didn't answer. Instead, I asked my own question.

"Do you think the spiritual truths coming from this dream text will be met with resistance?" I asked.

Fate

I turned to look at Pieta. His white teeth shined as he smiled. "What do you care?" he said. "You're going to go home and forget about this, right?"

I laughed. "Well, perhaps not. You've got my curiosity going now. I want to learn more about what this ancient dream has to say. I hope you'll fill me in as more of the interpretation becomes available."

We said goodbye, but I already knew I'd see Pieta again very soon.

It was late when I got home. Though I was tired, I walked onto my deck and considered how good my hot tub would feel. The evening was loud with dogs barking, and in the distance I could hear a leaf blower. The moon was peeking through the trees at the top of my property. It felt good to be back in my sanctuary.

The evening had been incredible. It had been a long time since I'd felt something this intuitive but real. I was hopeful that something new would make itself known to me about suffering. We certainly have had martyrdom and sacrifice burned into our psyches by the church. All of Western thought has been influenced by this perspective, whether people are aware of it or not. What if the church distorted the intent of these early spiritual teachings? What if spiritual growth and evolving consciousness is about understanding the relationship between the human spirit and ego—not fearing their relationship? As I readied for bed I thought, "Now, that's a refreshing possibility."

The next morning I woke up with a vigor that hadn't been there the day before.

"Huh," I thought. "Maybe the world and I are ready for a change after all."

The Astonishing Dream of JOB

Fate

1

Spiritual Truths

1. When the heart is convinced of truth we should not doubt it.
2. There is an ethical way to suffer.
3. Fear prevents the awareness that we are guided by our hearts.
4. Our story is driven by the human spirit: that which is around and through all that is.
5. We are angry at our predicament and don't know why.
6. Answer: we lose the capacity to distinguish between real and imagined fear.
7. Because our spirit is broken early we find it difficult to trust our feelings.
8. The injustice: we are destined to live in the fear and judgment of ego.
9. Feelings are more valid than thoughts.
10. Trusting our feelings validates the heart's intelligence.

The Astonishing Dream of JOB

2

The Comparison

After a good night's rest the hustle of the interstate was less daunting than usual and I arrived at my office with plenty of time to check my emails before my first client. When Pieta and I parted ways the night before, I let him know that I wanted to hear more. I was anxious for an email from him this morning, but he was notorious for baiting me like this and contacting me later.

As I settled onto my couch and drank my morning coffee, I felt my energy shift. I stretched out and closed my eyes and found that my mind was anything but quiet. Sifting through the conversation from the night before, I felt excited and curious. Who was this spiritual teacher Pieta had been talking to? And how did he know that this ancient dream was as valuable as he claimed it to be? The possibility that this text might confirm my research about our culture's view of compassion was very exciting to me. I had spent a career witnessing my patients' guilt block their recovery during trauma. Could it be that this ancient dream was the missing piece that would support my findings?

I am not a pessimist by nature, but I had spent enough time in the trenches with people to see their approach to a spiritual crisis during trauma. Many feel victimized by the event. I couldn't help but wonder how the average person would respond to learning that humans thirty-six hundred years ago were struggling in the same way. Would they be able to grasp that it was our early conditioning with adversity that detached us from the heart's wisdom? Would they accept that true compassion is not martyrdom and sacrifice, as has been taught by the church? It had been my life's work helping people see beyond their suffering as martyrs. Pieta's ancient dream may be the confirmation I needed to advance these concepts.

I sighed and closed my eyes. Focusing on my breathing, I drifted back and forth between my head and my heart. In the end, my heart wanted to give this new discovery a chance. It was not lost on me that this was perhaps exactly how Job resolved his own inner conflict.

My body relaxed as I let go of my concerns. I felt a warm wave of energy over-take me and I felt more at ease. Why had Pieta called me in the first place? Would he include me in whatever he was planning to do to get to the bottom of this discovery? Thinking about his smile and contagious enthusiasm, I knew that he wasn't baiting me without planning to include me. He just hadn't told me how—yet! Pieta had long been a trusted friend, counselor, and teacher. He was more experienced in spiritual matters, and would only advance my knowledge once he fostered some soul-searching. This had always been the nature of our relationship.

Knowing that my first client was coming soon, I got up and went into the coffee room for a refill. I noticed an older man speaking with one of the nurses, someone I didn't know. He glanced at me briefly, but continued speaking. He had a weathered outdoor look, leather skin from too much sun. He was probably only fifty-five or sixty, but his voice sounded older. He had an oddness about him that I couldn't

The Comparison

put my finger on. As I turned away, I heard part of the conversation.

"That's okay," the man said, "I just assumed you might have seen the paper today. Seems there's a lot of buzz on the internet about some kind of so-called ancient spiritual message from a dream that's been found. It's been ricocheting through the media today. They say it's a rumor, but even if it is, it's gaining a fair amount of momentum."

"Sounds interesting, for sure," the nurse said. "I'm always amazed by these kinds of rumors. Often, they turn out to be true and can really change how we look at ourselves." Stapling the man's information together, she placed it in a folder and filed it.

"I'll have to read it later," she said.

"Well, it wouldn't be the first time the press mindlessly leaped onto some new rumor, and it shed absolutely no light on the truth," the man continued.

Clearly needing to get to her next patient, the nurse cut their conversation short by handing him a card. "Here is your appointment card," she said, turning away from him. "You are scheduled to return in two weeks."

"Huh? Okay. Sure. Thanks," he said, seeming disappointed and turning to walk out the door.

I couldn't believe it. This new interpretation of the Book of Job was already hitting the rumor mill. I was so self-absorbed from yesterday's conversation that I hadn't even looked at a paper. Surely Pieta wouldn't have been so excited over a rumor. I lay back down on the couch. "Where is my first client?" I asked out loud. I was recalling what the nurse had said about discoveries such as the dream text changing how we look at ourselves. I totally agreed. The longer I rested there, the more the energy from the night before returned. I was eager to talk to someone about everything I was thinking. I was having trouble sitting still. Maybe the nurse had a copy of the paper. It was 10:15 a.m. My client was definitely a no-show.

Vacillating between last night's conversations and today's news, it was difficult to control my excitement. Not knowing what else to do with myself, I made my way to the nurse's station. She was busy with another patient. There was an empty chair close to her desk, so I sat and waited patiently for her to finish.

When her patient finally left, she stood and asked, "Can I help you?"

"Yes," I said sheepishly. "My name is Lou Costa. I work down the hall. I'm a psychologist here. I couldn't help but overhear you speaking earlier to a patient about an article in today's paper. The one you were talking to in the lobby? Did I hear correctly that the article was about an ancient text now considered a dream interpretation?"

"Yes, that's right," she said with a serene look on her face.

Although I had worked in this building for months, I had never seen this nurse before. I explained that a friend of mine had recently told me about the same rumors. Also, that I was surprised that the rumor was making the paper. She smiled and introduced herself as Carol Oxley, a temporary relief nurse for one of the residing doctors.

"Oh," I said. "That's why you didn't look familiar." I noticed that her next patient was getting impatient as he waited for his turn.

"I particularly liked what you said about such discoveries changing how we view ourselves. Have you actually seen the text?" I asked Carol.

"Oh my, you heard that?" she said surprised. "Our voices must really carry in this lobby. No. I didn't even know that

The Comparison

the story had made the paper," she laughed. "But, it turns out my husband does a lot of research in antiquities and old documents. He has shared some of what he's found out about it," she said. "Have you?"

"No," I confessed, "but my friend told me about the message." Her patient was looking at us sternly, trying to make eye contact with Carol.

Finally, she looked at him. "Excuse me, sir. Are you waiting for me? Would you mind if I get the other nurse to check you in?"

"Not at all," the man said.

Carol called out to one of her colleagues and nodded at the waiting patient.

At that point, Carol invited me into her office and closed the door behind her. "Tell me what you've heard about the dream's message," she said.

I paused for a moment, wrapping my mind around all that Pieta had told me the night before and trying to sort out what I understood about it.

"Well," I said. "It seems we went through a grave injustice when we began to acknowledge our feelings as more valid than emotions. In fact, the dream text suggests that feelings harshly judged by ego become emotions—anger. It turns out that viewing this ancient text as a dream reveals that the human heart has its own intelligence. My friend said the dreamer possessed a heart that was convinced of this intelligence. I guess what I've taken away from our conversation is that this text is an ancient representation of the birth of human feelings."

Saying all of this out loud felt weird and I stopped short and wondered if I had said too much.

The Astonishing Dream of JOB

Carol must have sensed my discomfort by the face I was making because she smiled and asked, "What do you think of that?"

"Well," I said. "I like that the text is making the distinction between feeling and emoting."

"Emotions certainly keep the psychiatric profession hopping," she said with a grin. "I've heard the psychiatrist in this building writes sixty-plus prescriptions a day! But of course I can understand how a text that professes to validate feelings would excite someone in the field of psychology."

I appreciated her observation and had to agree—the mental health model was broken. "Yes," I said. "We're learning that our feelings give us feedback about the quality of our thinking. Meanwhile, many of us are simply lost in our emotions. I agree with you, psychiatry continues to treat the symptoms."

"Well, that's the mental health profession for you," Carol said. Rather than teaching people how to utilize the kind of intelligence mentioned in this article, we offer them a quick fix and breed dependency on medications. It sounds like this idea of going with our heart's wisdom has merit. I know for me personally that it takes a lot to convince my heart that I'm wrong about something."

"Exactly," I agreed. "So, do you consider yourself intuitive or spiritual?" I asked.

"Oh, definitely spiritual," She answered. "My heart and I sorted that out a long time ago."

"So, you trust your heart when it comes to life matters?" I asked. "Especially, spiritual matters?"

"Yes! But you have to look at these things in a specific way." She took a deep breath, and then sighed. "I have been on the spiritual path a long time. I used to be stuck in the literal interpretation of biblical teachings. And I would never

The Comparison

question the church! I feel that has changed for me now. Maybe I've shifted from believing to knowing. My beliefs are up for discussion, but what my heart seems to know is not. That's certainly evidence of a heart that has matured, isn't it?"

"It sure is Carol," I said. "And it's my sense is that you're not alone in this shift."

"Well, I'd like to think I'm connected to my heart," she said smiling. "Especially since helping people is my profession."

"I am sure you're a wonderful nurse," I said.

"Thank you, Lou," she said agreeing. "So it's safe to say you are fascinated about this recent discovery?"

"Absolutely!" I said. "I think it is fascinating that we may be able to understand the people who predate religion and philosophy. What they were feeling and thinking about their world at the time. As a psychologist, I have grown to appreciate that each person's journey is different. But, when we speak of mankind, we're talking about a collective journey. The human experience isn't just about the gathering of facts. So much of what we believe about big life questions is based on so little. By getting in the heads, and in this case the hearts, of our predecessors we can see why we've turned out like we have. Maybe we can make sense of something that on the surface makes no sense."

"Well," she said. "My husband did say that this ancient biblical dream supports that the heart has intelligence."

"Yes," I said. "And, that's pretty exciting considering the age of the text. Science and medicine has just recently supported that the body has wisdom of its own, and now we may have access to a documented experience of someone who knew this three-thousand-six-hundred years ago."

The Astonishing Dream of JOB

When I asked Carol where her husband had gotten the information about the texts, she told me he'd come across it in his research—from a chat room about ancient discoveries. Apparently, the rumors were growing on the Internet. Maybe people's interest in the text was what had led the papers to run an article about it.

"From what I gather," she continued. "A bunch of folks could confirm the interpretation of Job's story existed, but many are afraid to talk about it. My husband told me that some members of the chat room had gotten threats from right-wing evangelicals and others who don't want people tampering with biblical scripture. This kind of stuff excites my husband," she said blushing. "I already have too much to worry about with my patients, and very little time as it is. I can put you in touch with him."

"Really!" I said, excited. "Do you think he would meet with me?"

"Sure," she said. "He lives for this stuff." She paused.

"One thing my heart has taught me," she said, "is that there are no coincidences in spiritual work. We met today, I believe, so that you could meet my husband. In fact, tomorrow is my last day here. Imagine that!"

"I agree." I said. "Something larger certainly seems to be directing me."

She smiled. "I'll give you his number, hold on a second." She walked toward her desk, presumably to write down the number.

I could not believe what was happening. One day I was speaking of a recovered dream text with a dear friend, and the next day threads of information about it are connecting lives of total strangers. I hoped that Carol's husband was as pleasant as she was "Okay," she said, returning to where I

The Comparison

was standing. "Here it is. I'll call him and let him know to be expecting your call. His name is Chris."

Thanking her, I exited her office and moved back into the waiting room. I knew now that I was going to have to clear my schedule to meet with Chris. When I went back to my office, my secretary informed me that my 11:00 a.m. client had called to cancel as well. I couldn't help but wonder if my clients were canceling to make room for me to learn more about this discovery. Coincidence? Or, was the Universe allowing these events to unfold as they were?

I called Chris immediately and asked if we could meet at the local public library that afternoon. He was eating an early lunch, and agreed to meet forty-five minutes later. I grabbed a salad on the way and got to the library early; waiting for a man who fit the description he gave me: tall, with brown hair, and wearing a blue jacket.

He arrived fifteen minutes after I got there. He was a serious-looking man and right away I could tell he was the inquisitive type.

"Hello," he said shaking my hand. "I'm Chris. Carol told me you've got the scent for this rewritten copy of the Book of Job. I just discovered that the entire book, all forty-two chapters, had been interpreted as a dream a week ago. But already the number of people asking and searching about it online is staggering."

"What can you tell me about the interpretation? I mean, what does it say exactly?" I asked.

"You have to understand," he said. "I don't have access to anyone who has seen the text directly. I can only tell you what I've heard. I know a little bit about the beginning messages."

"Whatever you can share," I said. "I want to learn more about the heart's intelligence, but I also want more details about Job's experience."

He smiled. "You're a researcher-investigator type, I see."

"Absolutely. Tell me what you know."

"All I ask in the telling is that you not try to understand it. Instead, attempt to feel the message. It is coming from the deepest recesses of the human psyche. To grasp its meaning, you must put yourself in the reality of the person who lived the experience. It's taken thirty-six hundred years for us to find how we lost the integrity of our heart's intelligence, so to understand where we are today; we must look back at when it happened."

"How do I do that?"

"I'll do my best to guide you."

I was initially a little nervous about what I was about to hear, but I looked into Chris's reassuring eyes and said, "Okay, I'm ready to try."

"Are you familiar with guided meditation?" he asked.

"Yes I am." I answered. "Why?"

"Well, I want you to close your eyes," Chris instructed. "Imagine that you are living in a time of no worries. In fact, you have little experience with your emotions at all. Then suddenly, one day when you least expect it, fear and judgment enter your reality. You know this because for the first time your emotions warn you about it. Afraid and unsure of what you've just experienced, you introvert to self-protect. You have suddenly begun the road less traveled—the inner journey.

"Now," he continued, "inside the unconscious, the soul provides you an above perspective—or objective view—of your inner world. Objective, in this context, means a

The Comparison

detached or distant observation that is without bias or prejudice. Seeing what the soul sees, certain aspects of the self come into your awareness. Specifically, you witness an interaction between the ego and human spirit. As an observer, you can only see what is happening, but can't stop it. The ego asks the spirit, "Where did you come from?" Spirit answers, "I am around and through all that is."

"Wait," I said. "The dream distinguishes the interaction between the ego and human spirit?"

"Yes," Chris said. "And that is not all. Because of this interpretation, the reader also gets to witness the effect these two qualities had on the emotional self. In fact, my sense is that the observation is multi-dimensional."

"How so," I asked.

"The Book of Job interpreted as a dream," he said, "gives us a personal and collective journaling of an emotional catharsis. We get to witness the effect on the individual and we get the hint of the maturation on future generations."

I remembered what Pieta had said: The Book of Job may represent the birth of recorded feelings. Could it be that the dream text was our first record of an emotional catharsis?

"What an amazing vantage point—to be able to see these relationships unfold through Job's experience and the interpreter's words!" I said. "What exactly is the relationship between the human spirit and ego?"

"Simply put," he said. "The human spirit, by design, is intended to provoke an emotional reaction from the ego."

Pieta had spoken about this last night. Job was minding his own business when one day two deities decide to play roulette with his life. Satan bet God that Job, though righteous, had a weakness. He accused God of overprotecting Job and his wealth. Essentially, Satan bet that Job only served God because he was a man of material possessions. As Chris spoke, I was beginning to realize that understanding Job's text as a dream relayed this bet in a wholly different light: it actually symbolized the human spirit provoking the ego to create an emotional reaction—fear. On a personal level, it provides us an opportunity to see if fear will create anger and break us down. On a collective level, we get to see if the experience of suffering will break us open. One is suffering for the self as victim; the other is suffering with the self as maturity and transformation.

"I've heard of this part before," I said.

"Well, as you can imagine," he said. "When life is going along as it should, and then for no good reason all hell breaks loose, something has to give. In an emotional state of despair, Job became terrified. In his confusion, he decided that the ego was fickle—it gives and takes whenever it chooses. And, though this was going on inside of him—and inside of us all the time—he couldn't initially question it! Largely because in that moment; he was detached from the objectivity and compassion of his heart."

"It makes sense to me that these were the tests of Job or the individual, but what is the collective message in his experience?"

"That is a great question," he said. "It turns out that the experience of the emotional self is meant to suffer us awake."

"Awake to what?" I asked.

"Consciousness," he answered. "Job was becoming aware of the relationship between his mind and the world around him. He was experiencing his feelings fully awake. If he remained unconscious or unaware, he would be at the mercy of his emotions."

"So," I asked. "Suffering with ourselves awake the emotional-self matures?"

The Comparison

"Yes, yes! Awake enough that we can begin to question our fate and the role of the ego as it relates with spirit. Importantly, we learn that the human spirit actually intends for us to wake up. The ego does not budge without the spirit's provocation."

"The spirit's provocation, what does that mean?" I asked.

"The ego is permitting the suffering, but the spirit is orchestrating the suffering. It begins the process of connecting us to our heart. But something else has to happen first."

Following everything that Chris was saying felt like having an X-ray of what was going on inside a human being while they were suffering. I could feel myself trembling in anticipation of what he was going to say next.

"What is that?" I asked.

"We have yet to understand the inner voices that plague us during our suffering," he said.

"You are kidding me!" I exclaimed. "This dream interpretation distinguishes the inner voices of Job's suffering as well? I assume these are separate from the constructs of ego and spirit?"

"Yes. I don't have much information about it yet," Chris said, "but I have heard rumors that there are several verses of the dream specific to Job's inner conversation. Thus far, we have been learning about personality dynamics (ego) and the energy (spirit) that animates this personality. What's coming is actual self-talk, or evidence of Job's thinking at the time. Imagine the understanding and compassion this might make possible for the world."

"Yes," I said. "I can imagine the impact on individuals wanting to understand their inner life. This stuff is amazing. The world gets unheard of evidence that there is an important relationship between the human spirit and personality development. They are not separate or in opposition to one another. Nor do they stay abstract or theoretical. In truth, they actually work together to bring the individual into the present, in spite of any adversity the person might have undergone. Now you are telling me that we might get examples of self-talk during suffering. It's as if we are finding a prescription for what to expect when facing adversity, as well as the best way to endure it and grow."

"Indeed it is," Chris answered. "And our longing for relief from such suffering was initially a longing for love. Love in this context was freedom to be and something we thought we had in the beginning, but then somehow lost."

"So, what can we say that Job has learned thus far in his emotional journey?" I asked.

"The dream implies it is his and our fate to hear inner judgments and to become afraid—of being afraid," he answers.

"That's paranoia," I said. "My God, that is the actual state of our culture now."

I paused, taking everything in. I couldn't believe that I was here, having a conversation about something that happened thirty-six hundred years ago, and yet finding in it something that was still so relevant today. I also realized how rare this analysis was—that we were speaking of an ancient person's inner personality traits as opposing forces—each moving him to a place of healing and understanding.

"So," I started, trying to formulate my next question. "There is a prescriptive tone or a 'how to suffer' quality represented by Job's experience, yes?"

"I think the prescription is forming," he said. "At a minimum we are learning that it is important to not passively serve the ego. Self-examination and inquiry are important first steps to understanding how to suffer."

The Comparison

"I can see that now," I said. "Also, that suffering needs to be done with compassion or we fall victim to our emotions?"

"Yes," he answered. "And, we also have an answer for 'why' we suffer—to become conscious. Essentially, what we see happening inside of Job is the human spirit provoking a heartfelt question: are feelings or intuitions as important, or equal to, the ego's judgments? By asking this question we see the first hint that mirrors the problems in contemporary spirituality," he said.

I understood what Chris was saying—that Job was questioning which was above the other: ego or feelings? I understood ego to be that part of the psyche that experiences the external world, or reality. By using our senses, it organizes our thoughts and governs our actions. Ego is a survival mechanism that mediates between our impulses and the demands of the environment. It gets its standards from the culture and is tied to the brain. In contrast, feeling is an immediate reaction to the present moment, and the instrument used for its perception is the body and heart.

"What is our contemporary spiritual problem?" I asked.

"No one wants to admit, let alone work through, the abusive and powerful influence of the human ego. Instead, we think there is some shortcut around it. This dream text shows that Job decided to do just the opposite."

"Are the emotional and spiritual self above the ego?" I asked out loud. "The average person spends the majority of their life buffing, polishing, and worshipping the ego. It usually isn't until life hits them between the eyes with something that they wake up to the spiritual. And, even then, not everyone stays awake."

"Sadly, it's this unconscious allegiance to ego that plagues the human race today," Chris said. "If given an option to

The Astonishing Dream of JOB

worship love or fear, many choose fear. Sorting out Job's dilemma could be an important first step in turning this around in our culture. If only?" With that, he sighed.

Suddenly, a noise from the back of the library caught Chris's attention and he turned away. I could tell by the sadness in his eyes that he was moved by our discussion, but it was also clear that it was coming to an end.

"Thank you so much!" I said.

"Hey, no problem." he replied. "At this point, we are just at the tip of the iceberg. There is so much to this teaching left to decipher. I hope to learn more as the week's progress."

We both checked our watches and commented that we couldn't believe how long we had been talking. We agreed to stay in touch and then walked in opposite directions toward our cars. I wondered how much of the information I'd just received, Pieta had heard—and couldn't wait to discuss it with him.

The conversations thus far were beginning to have some continuity. It was possible—likely even—that Job had a natural external experience that he interpreted as God. His story—as a dream—was interpreting these events as an internal struggle with what was happening to him as the result of a severe storm. I decided to return to my office and call Pieta if he hadn't already been in touch by email.

The Comparison

2

Spiritual Truths

11. The truth about suffering is stored in the human psyche.
12. We knew about the heart's intelligence 3600 years ago.
13. Fear and judgment introvert a portion of the ego to self-protect.
14. Ego and spirit shape this as the emotional-self.
15. The human spirit provokes us for a feeling re-action.
16. Instead, we re-enact or emote the initial suffering.
17. We are to question the relationship between ego and spirit OR passively submit.
18. The ego permits suffering; the spirit provokes it; while the soul wants the experience to connect us to our hearts.
19. We must 'let go' of ego to know love.
20. Understanding why we are afraid of being afraid IS the spiritual journey.

The Astonishing Dream of JOB

3

Voices

Pieta showed up at my home early Saturday morning with an urgency I had not seen from him in a long time. He wanted me to shower, pack enough clothes for a week, and told me we would leave immediately. I did as he asked without asking questions. Other than telling we were going to Jericho, Israel, he gave me no other details. We drove in silence for most of the way to the airport. I asked him several questions about our destination, but he told me all of my questions would be answered once we got there.

One advantage of being from a small town is that the airports are never busy. We were able to get through the baggage check and onto the plane with little interference. By noon, we were already well on our way. We ate a small lunch, washed it down with some wine, and read up on Jericho.

Turns out Jericho is believed to be one of the oldest cities in the world. It was the first city captured by the Israelites after their forty years of wandering in the desert and their exodus from Egypt. Jericho and the Gaza Strip were the first territories given to the Palestinians by Israel as part of the 1994 peace agreement. Jericho sits between Mt. Nebo in the east, the Central Mountains to the west, and the Dead Sea to the south. I knew that Job's experience took place nearby, and that this trip surely had to do with digging up more information about these texts.

Hours later, on the decent into Damascus International Airport, Pieta told me we would be spending the first night, 143 kilometers away, in Akko, Israel, one of the oldest cities in the world. "In fact," he said, "it was first mentioned in written records of Egyptian hieroglyphs in 3500 BC." There was a rabbi he wanted to meet, and we'd be heading out to Ramhal Synagogue the next day.

When collecting our rental car, they told us we were about twenty kilometers from the city center. Pieta had reserved us a room at the Art House on the north-eastern side of Damascus. The drive gave us a chance to unwind from the flight and we went to bed shortly after checking in.

After a restless night's sleep, we woke up early to make our way to Ramhal Synagogue, a tiny house of prayer off the main street of Akko's colorful Old City Market. The synagogue was named after the Italian sage Rabbi Moshe Haim Luzatto, known by his acronym the Ramhal. He arrived in Akko in 1743 AD. A controversial figure for his time, Ramhal is now recognized as a brilliant mystic and ethicist. I asked Pieta more questions on the drive to the synagogue, but again he asked me to wait.

From the car I could hear the waves of the Mediterranean Sea crashing against the walls of this old but beautiful city. The literature they gave us at the airport said that these steep, thick sandstone walls had survived centuries of the sea's wrath. I also learned Akko was an important city in ancient times. The Crusaders captured it and the Ottomans lived here for centuries. Even Napoleon Bonaparte tried to conquer Akko, but after two months of siege and failed attempts to storm the city's walls, he was said to have retreated in humiliation.

Voices

When we got out of the vehicle, Pieta hesitated and looked at the surrounding buildings. Among the high-walled alleys we could see a huge mosque and a Christian monastery. The city was full of intriguing museums and old churches, and its central feature was a fishing port.

"I'm going to speak to the Rabbi at that mosque," Pieta told me. "Would you mind if I left you to yourself for a while? You're going to love this city."

"Ancient architecture and old churches," I acquiesced. "What's not to love?"

As he started to walk away, he paused and turned to me. "Be sure to check out the tunnels of the Knights Templar. I'll catch up with you at dinnertime." We established a nearby meeting place and he turned to make his way to the mosque.

I knew Pieta was keeping me in the dark on purpose, so I wasn't concerned. He had his way of doing things, and I'd long ago learned not to question his methods. I knew I would find out what I wanted to know, so it was just a matter of keeping my anticipation in check. He had already told me that the spiritual teacher he was working with wanted to remain anonymous, and what better place in the world to keep a secret than Israel. Anywhere but here the significance of Job's story interpreted as a dream was likely a touchy subject. There is a minority view among the rabbis of the Talmud that Job never even existed. In this view, Job was a literary creation by a prophet who wanted to convey a divine message. I remembered reading somewhere that the Talmud goes to great lengths to ascertain when Job actually lived. It seems that in Israel the debate over Job's message is ongoing.

I stood in the closest shade I could find near where we'd parked the car. As I was reading a local brochure, a voice from behind asked, "It's a fascinating place, isn't it?"

The Astonishing Dream of JOB

I turned quickly. A woman in her late thirties, pushing a bicycle, stood behind me. She had dark hair and dark eyes. She looked at me as if we were familiar and I wondered if she had just been in the mosque that Pieta had entered.

"It's unbelievable!" I said. "You can smell the history in the air."

Between the ancient alleyways was a lively open market humming with activity. It was early Sunday afternoon now, and I imagined it was probably one of the busiest times.

"I've heard that this market is home to one of Israel's most famous hummus restaurants," she said. "Even parties of two have to wait in line for a table here."

I smiled. "Do you happen to know where the Knights Templar tunnels are?" I asked.

"I think I just biked past that area of town," she said. "If you walk with me I'm sure I can backtrack."

After introducing ourselves, we walked down the sidewalk and onto the ancient streets to the south. Her name was Zoe Hacket, and if she hadn't told me she was an American tourist, I would have thought she was a local. We walked for several minutes before she confirmed my assumption that she had just been attending a conference at the mosque. I wondered if she had been meeting with the same person as Pieta.

"Have you been to Akko before?" she asked.

"No, I haven't," I replied." Sadly, I only know what I've recently read about the place in a brochure."

"Well, this is my second trip. About a year ago, some new information about The Dead Sea Scrolls was circulating through Akko. They're said to be the oldest known surviving copies of the Bible. Spiritual enthusiasts were trickling in to explore the rumors—teachers and their students mainly.

Then, last month …" She hesitated for an instant and looked at me. "Have you heard about an ancient dream interpretation that has been associated with the Book of Job?"

"Yes, I have," I replied. "In fact, that's why I'm here. But I've just heard about the general theme of the message." I proceeded to tell her that the friend I was traveling with had just made his way to the conference at the mosque.

"Then it seems we are on the same quest," she said smiling. "I knew you being at this particular mosque was no coincidence."

We had come to a short wall overlooking the marketplace and we stopped there. "Oh yeah, why is that?" I asked.

She leaned her bicycle against the wall and smiled. "There are few places in Akko one can ask about Job's dream interpretation. This mosque is one of them. Besides, Akko is fast becoming a gathering place for spiritual teachers and their followers who are seeking to understand Job's predicament."

"Tell me a little more about the conference," I prompted.

"We mostly talked about Job's inner voice," she said.

"I don't know anything about that," I said.

"It describes how deep within the unconscious there is a synthesis or integration occurring designed to make him whole. The Rabbi told us that the initial three characters in the dream include the ego, spirit, and the emotional-self."

"Yes," I said. "My friend and I have discussed this portion several times."

"Well, I'm not as clear about the interaction of these elements as I'd like to be," she said. "What is your take on it?"

The Astonishing Dream of JOB

"My understanding is that Job's heart is conflicting with what is happening to him," I said. "And, his ego is being influenced by the human spirit for the sole purpose of stirring his emotions. Essentially, we are getting to observe an ancient spiritual trial—from the inside out. We also learn that even though his heart says otherwise, he gives into these trials in despair."

"That's a good summary," she said. "And, by observing from the inside out, you mean we are getting to witness the interaction of these inner qualities IN Job—because of the dream text?"

"Exactly!" I answered. "Do the teachers you've come into contact with think this inner dimension is worth understanding? Most people believe the unconscious is a vague theory rather than an aspect of the human experience worth acknowledging."

"I think most do," she said. "I'm certainly one that does. Of course, there will be religious literalists who will be uncomfortable with someone reinterpreting the Bible."

"So, you're a teacher then?" I asked.

"Yes," she answered. "I am a transpersonal psychologist with a small practice in California. We are a group of psychologists that concern ourselves with the study of humanity's highest potential. We teach recognition, understanding, and the realization of spiritual and transcendent states of consciousness. Some people accuse us of practicing psychiatry without a license, but Job's 'inside world' is very real to us."

I was amazed how much Zoe and I had in common, my orientation and training as a psychologist being very similar to hers.

"The Rabbi at the mosque said the better we understand the interaction of these initial three qualities, the better we can relate to Job's self-talk." At this Zoe paused, perhaps to see if I wanted to hear more. I motioned with my hand for her to continue.

"Well," she continued. "My understanding is that Job is skeptical about why he is being tested. Also, that the reasons for the trials are eluding or confusing him. Meanwhile, his heart is screaming for him to question everything. Is that your sense as well?"

"Yes," I agreed. "Essentially, we are learning that Job wanted to trust his instincts. It seems that the dream interpretation is preparing us for more examples of how Job may be speaking to himself. At least, that's my take."

"I agree," Zoe answered. "The Rabbi told me that Job is being challenged by his logic, his inner critic, and his emotions as he sorts out what the heart feels."

"So Job's inner dialogue demonstrates how emotions can contaminate our thinking?" I said. "That reminds me of the movie: 'What the (Bleep) Do We Know?'[2] Have you seen it? It suggests that a thought goes nowhere without an electrical charge—emotion. Also, that the intent of that thought can impact our physical health."

"Yes! That movie was a classic! I especially liked the research of Masaru Emoto[3], the man interested in the molecular structure of water who wanted to know if it would respond to nonphysical events. Do you remember? He set up a series of studies, applied positive and negative mental stimuli, and then photographed the result with a dark field microscope."

"Yes, I remember that," I said. "But I forgot how he measured the mental piece."

"He printed out words and taped them to bottles of distilled water. Then, he left them out overnight. The next morning he froze the water and examined the formation of water crystals. He wanted to see if the crystals would form differently based on the words intent."

"Now I remember," I said. "He spoke of intention as the driving force that changed the molecular structure of the water."

"Exactly," she continued. "Turns out the negative words barely formed crystals while the positive words were almost perfectly symmetrical. It's fascinating when you consider that our bodies are predominantly made up of water."

"Yeah," I smiled. "Emoto's research makes you wonder if thoughts can do that to water, then what are our thoughts doing to us."

"Absolutely." she said. "It is very popular these days to use energy in a general way to refer to all of the intentions in our mind and spirit. In fact, many folks merge spiritual and mental energy, saying that they are just two different kinds of energies. In truth, they correspond to each other. If what the Rabbi suggested is true, we are getting an opportunity to see how Job's thoughts are affecting his body."

"By correspondence do you mean that what is happening to Job externally versus what he is actually saying or doing to himself?" I asked.

"Yes," she answered excited. "Isn't that incredible?"

I was impressed by Zoe's depth of knowledge and how well read she seemed to be. It made me think about my small town and the lack of like-minded people around me—and it made me want to listen to her forever.

"Your understanding of all of this is fascinating," I said. "Please go on."

"Well," she continued. "What the Bleep goes on to tell us that things in the world are spread-out fields that act in a unified way to give one actual outcome. For example, when humans think, we have an intention that considers many different possibilities, and then acts on one of them. Life operates the same way, and what we are seeing is that physical nature is no different. It is not conscious of itself in the same way, but it contains the same kinds of processes, the same functions. The natural corresponds to the physical, and we see how everything is joined together."

"How is this reflected in Job's self-talk?" I asked.

"We know that there is a correspondence between the functions in quantum nature: energy and matter and the functions in the mind: thought and intention. Emoto's research suggests that they might not be the same in substance, but the functional patterns are the same. This would mean for Job that the body couldn't tell whether he was having an inside or outside experience. So, interpreting what was happening to him as an 'inside' experience—as a dream—is valid, and also has wonderful spiritual implications."

"What that means to me spiritually is that he is physically becoming the very words he is saying to himself. Is that the implication?"

"Yes, yes!" Zoe said, excited. "In his moment of despair, he is laden with a variety of emotions, each one fueling his confusion and thinking. Referencing Emoto's research, imagine that Job is resisting becoming the negative things he is emoting and instead is trying to honor his feelings."

"And," I responded, "if not for using his heart as a compass, he would have been lost to these emotions?"

"Yes! That is exactly what is happening to him initially. Because the human heart is tied to intent and truth, it's almost like his heart is stalling to give him time to ask questions."

The Astonishing Dream of JOB

"Now that is amazing," I said. "The heart's intent—interfering with faulty logic."

"My sense," she continued, "is that Job is attempting to manage his emotions by feeling in a purposeful way. He somehow knew that feeling was the power of emotion merged with the guidance of the human heart. The Book of Job, interpreted as a dream, offers us spiritual depth that is not easily seen in the Bible's version. His story as myth, or even as literal or biblical history, does not give us such valuable spiritual information."

"Wow," I said. "Purposeful suffering, believe it or not, this has been the focus of my work with severe trauma patients for years now. I often teach: feel more and emote less."

"Well, it seems you were onto something," she said supportively. "Unfortunately, too many people look at these ancient biblical texts as the writings of God, believing that to view them in any other way are unacceptable. To me, this is like going into a restaurant and instead of eating the food, people literally eat the menu. The depth of many world religions is not in the book per se, but in between the lines or behind the words."

"You mean through metaphor and symbols?" I asked.

"Yes," she answered. "The Job story uses the metaphor of a storm to throw him in on himself so we can witness what turns out to be—an awakening."

Just then our conversation was interrupted by a voice calling out from a distance. "Hey Zoe, is that you?" Standing in line at one of the market restaurants below us waving, tall and wearing a backpack, he looked as if he had just come from a hike.

"My friend is holding me a place in line," Zoe said. "I need to go let them know what I am doing. I'll be right back.

Voices

I have my notes on Job's struggle with his self-talk in my friend's backpack. Maybe we can find a copy machine in one of the local Internet cafes."

"That would be great!"

As she walked down the landing to meet her friend, I reviewed everything we'd just discussed. I couldn't wait to share it all with Pieta.

Returning with a spiral notebook, Zoe handed over her notes and pointed out a nearby café. I'll be at the restaurant when you're finished."

I took the notebook and walked around the corner as Zoe had instructed. The café was relatively empty and there was a single copy machine in the corner.

I was so excited to read Zoe's notes that I didn't start copying immediately. Instead, I purchased a soft drink and sat for a few minutes leafing through the pages.

Zoe had labeled the first page of her notes as "Job's Self-Talk." My hands were sweating as I read the first entry:

"The dream interpretation of the Book of Job implies that his inner voices — labeled as friends Eliphaz the Themanite, Baldad the Suhite, and Sophar the Naamathite— are strictly internal characters and distinctly different in their presentation and intent. One attempts to guide and support, the other argues and condemns, and the third tries to reach a compromise the other two do not."

I read this over several times trying to take in what she had written. This must have been what she had discussed with the Rabbi. She had said that the dream interpretation was preparing us for how Job was speaking to himself. Three friends equaled three inner voices? Then I came to a phrase in Zoe's notes that caused a lump to form in my throat:

The Astonishing Dream of JOB

"If we are not nourished (by love) there is yearning, and there is an accompanying fateful noise. In this way, the emotional-self becomes afraid of being afraid."

"Yearning has a fateful noise?" I thought to myself. "Is this the sequence of our internal chatter: supportive, condemning, and compromising. Chatter that we all have to live with? Sometimes the volume of all three being so loud that self-love is drowned out? Yearning for relief, we become afraid of being afraid? I wondered if this was the volume that psychiatry was attempting to lower with medications."

As I thought about this, I heard Zoe entered the café. I had already been sitting for an hour and I hadn't made a single copy.

"Isn't this a quaint café?" she asked as she approached. "So, I see you've done little copying." She smiled. "Hard to put down once you start reading, isn't it?"

"Yes, and I've barely gotten past the first few pages," I said. "I was just sitting here pondering the description of Job's inner voices. Fascinating."

"Three voices to be exact: one that supports, and one that condemns, and a third that seeks compromise." She said.

"I have to say, this is pretty amazing considering that many psychological theories of personality are broken down into three constructs like this." I said.

Zoe smiled. "I wondered if you would catch that."

"Yes," I laughed. "Pretty amazing considering Freud's Id, Ego, and Super Ego."

"Don't forget Eric Byrne's Parent, Adult, Child ego states." She said.

"I know, I know," I said excited. "Thirty-six hundred years ago. You've got to be kidding me. Job's story as a dream is giving us a crash course in personality development, absolutely amazing."

"It really is," she agreed. "My mentor told me that the three voices make more sense the further you get into the text interpretation."

"What is your sense of this first voice?"

"I will do my best to tell you what my teacher told me. The first character or voice we get to examine is the supportive one. Because of this self-talk, Job is realizing that emotions have a purpose, they are set to memory, and they cause us to re-enact or relive certain things."

"Hmmm, that is consistent with recent research about cell memory," I said. "Cells do not remember thoughts, but instead remember metabolism or brain chemistry. Emotions are biochemical."

"Yes," she said. "And an unbalanced emotion like anger will feed on itself, giving energy to thoughts of self-judgment. This is what Job is doing in his experience, and it is also what we do when we get angry at ourselves. The text tells us that anger diminishes if you don't feed it."

"Do you have more about this in your notes?" I asked. "That's a curious statement."

"Yes, yes," she answered taking her notebook and flipping the pages. "Hold on. It should be right here."

Handing the spiral notebook back to me, Zoe pointed to a passage. "This is what the Rabbi gave me."

"The inner voice of constructive criticism," I read aloud.

"It is true that emotions can teach and make us stronger. Its re-enactments of injustice can confirm us when we are off balance. They can even bring us courage when our ground is weak. But, the punishment you resist is the result of your own making.

The Astonishing Dream of JOB

There is the submission and tolerance of before. Ask yourself, when change ever happens to the innocent? You must be guilty. When has the heart's perspective been the final word? Emotions out of balance feed on themselves and end up submitting to ego judgments anyway. The voice of a martyr is broken by the ego's aggression."

"Hmm," I said closing the notebook. "I see what you meant about the constructive criticism of this particular voice. Don't fear and love fuel our dreams when we sleep anyway?" I asked.

"Yes," she replied, "but it is more accurate to say that opposite emotions or energies like fear/love, shame/pride, guilt/innocence, or anger/letting go, activate our dreams. Opposing energies in the body, projected onto the mind, is what causes us to dream. Job's experience caused nightmares and prevented him for being able to sleep. The dream text says: "Anger seizes us so that we tremble down to our bones and it causes the hair on our necks to rise."

"So, the more intense the opposition, the more intense the dream?" I asked.

"Yes, the degree or intensity of these opposing energies can create nightmares." She answered.

"That's certainly been my experience with trauma patients," I said, "that the soul orchestrates the dream for the individual to see something they are ignoring internally. Do you agree with that?"

"Of course that makes sense," she answered. "When you consider that dreams are simply a long-distance phone call from the unconscious, the louder the ring the more intense the need to pick up the receiver."

"That fits what the dream text is saying about Job's sleepless nights."

Voices

"Yes, the whole thing is amazing," Zoe continued. "It's hard to believe, but when we are talking about Job's nightmares, we actually are looking at this material as a dream within a dream. One the interpreter, the other the dreamer himself—Job."

Zoe exhibited the same passion on this subject that Pieta did, and I felt myself getting even more excited about sharing her notes with him.

"There is a profound point in the dream interpretation," she said, "where Job is asked if the ego and the individual can be compared to each other. Or, are they one and the same? His inner voice warns that they cannot: 'Anyone that is grounded in such a belief will be consumed like a moth to flame.' Isn't that amazing?"

"You're the one that's amazing," I said.

She looked at me with a sheepish smile. "Well, thank you. I find it all very fascinating. More than anything I just have a deep understanding of personality and ego disorder."

"Well, I am certainly impressed." I said. "I understand personality theory, but you seem to have a symbolic understanding that I lack."

"Thank you," she said. "I see personality disorder as an enduring pattern of inner experiences and behaviors that deviate markedly from the expectations of the culture of the individual who exhibits them."

"Expectations of the culture?" I asked.

"Yes, look at what is happening to Job. He is undergoing an external experience that throws him inside the self. In an effort to understand, he questions, argues, attacks, emotes, and struggles with himself. He knows that what he is experiencing is inconsistent with what he knows in his heart to be true. He is an individual divided against himself."

"That is a great definition of personality disorder—a person divided against themselves," I replied.

"So he's begging for guidance?" I asked.

"He's praying," she explained. "He wants to understand the 'why' and 'how' of his predicament. He is reaching deeper and deeper for the answer."

I must have looked puzzled because she laughed, but then said seriously, "Perhaps we should take a break so you can make your copies. You're barely getting anything else done today."

I moved to the copy machine and thanked Zoe for taking the time to explain the dream interpretation as she saw it, and for showing me around Akko.

"Hey, we seekers need to stick together," she said smiling. "I am happy to help. At some level we all have a responsibility to understand this ancient message and bring it to the world. It may or may not be new, but it is certainly reinforcing what is lacking in the spiritual movement: heart."

After I was finished copying, we gathered our stuff and walked outside. Immediately we ran into a couple trying to get our attention. "Excuse me, please!"

A man and a woman were walking quickly up the cobblestone street toward us. They appeared to be in their late forties, American, and dressed more formally than typical tourists.

"Could one of you tell us how to get to the Ramhal Synagogue?" the man asked.

"Sure," Zoe answered cautiously. "Are you investigating the rumors about the newly discovered biblical texts?" she asked.

"Huh? What? Uh, yes," the man stuttered. "My wife and I were attending a local parish and everyone there was talking about it. We are conservative Christians and concerned about the implications of such a document."

"Sounds as though you're worried about a different truth being revealed," Zoe said smiling. She was calm as still water, but it was clear to me that she was provoking them to leave.

"We think it is absurd that people actually believe that some new, mysterious transcript that claims the Book of Job was just a dream is true," the woman said. "No one has ever said this before."

"Have you read any of the document or the messages the new interpretation might reveal?" Zoe asked.

The man ignored her question and asked again, "Can you tell us how to get to the Ramhal Synagogue?"

"Of course," Zoe said. "You're looking for a red building that is close to the fishing pier at the end of the market. I think it is an old meeting hall. The synagogue is right beside it. You should find what you're looking for there."

"Thank you," the woman said as she hurried her husband along.

"That's not directions to the synagogue."

"Yeah, you caught that?" she replied. "I thought I would spare the Rabbi some time. I know he is quite busy speaking with supporters and would appreciate avoiding the naysayers."

"So you've made yourself his personal screener?" I laughed. "Where did you send them anyway?"

"It is the site of an old church, and the pastor there is great when it comes to conservatives like those two. We get people like them through here occasionally, and not just religious folks, but curiosity seekers as well—people who can't begin to grasp the significance of this discovery."

The Astonishing Dream of JOB

I nodded. I hadn't considered that there may be those seeking to discredit the dream text in Akko as well.

"Here come some people you might want to meet," Zoe said, pointing toward the alley. "Follow me."

Zoe introduced me to Rachel and Bruce, explaining that they were specifically interested in the messages of Job's self-talk. Bruce spoke with me for a few minutes before saying he needed to return to his hotel for a nap. Rachel, a teacher, was eager to answer my questions.

"You're seekers as well?" I asked excited.

She gave me a broad smile. I knew my enthusiasm could be contagious. "Yes," she answered. "Just like Zoe, we're fascinated by all of this. We're still examining the portion of the self-talk that is supposed to be comforting Job. Are you familiar with what is happening at this section of the dream?" I shook my head. "Job is minding his own business when some external event happens. As he experiences the external influences, he turns inside himself to reflect upon the circumstances he faces."

"Yes, the initial circumstances that set up his inner predicament," I answered. "I was just reading about that in Zoe's notes."

"Well then," she said. "Did her notes say anything about Job being asked to go to a deeper place of virtue?"

"No," I answered. "I did not see that in her materials. What does that mean?"

"Well, the human spirit is provoking a heartfelt question for Job," she continued. "Are feelings or intuitions as important, or equal to, the ego's judgments?"

"Oh yes!" I replied, remembering my previous conversation with Chris in the States. "I am aware of that passage."

"Anyway, he is examining the impact of what it means to be emotional," she said.

"Can you give me an example?" I asked.

"He is learning about how anger can affect our common sense and judgment. Also, how resentment and envy can rob us of our innocence. But, it's the accompanying insight in this section that is unbelievable. It is consistent with what we are learning in physics. Are you familiar with Masura Emoto's work with intention and vibration?"

"Yes, yes," I answered. "Zoe and I were just talking about that."

At that point Zoe stood up and said she had to go. She gave each of us a hug.

"Lou, I think Rachel can answer your questions from here. I'm sure we'll see each other again around Akko before you leave. This town is too small."

"I can't thank you enough, Zoe," I said. "This is turning out to be an incredible day. I was worried about Pieta leaving me, but I couldn't imagine the day going any better."

After Zoe left, Rachel picked right back up where she'd left off. "Back to Emoto's research," she said. "If you remember, his claims were that human consciousness has an effect on the molecular structure of water."

"Yes," I said. "His research is very profound, for sure. Do you see some correlation with what Job is saying to himself?"

"Yes! We get an additional insight into Job's reaction."

"How so?" I asked.

"Because nothing happens in the universe without an accompanying vibration or intention, Job's sadness does not come out of nowhere," she answered.

The Astonishing Dream of JOB

"Yes, go on," I said.

"Remember, Job is trying to resolve the question: Are human beings born to suffer or are they born to be spiritually free?" Rachel said. "Of course, if we leave this up to the judgment of ego, the answer is that we are born to suffer. Job knows in his heart that this is not the truth."

"Yes, I remember now. You are referring to the part in What the Bleep about energy fields and how the body is actually an antenna within these fields."

"Exactly!" she replied. "Remember what it said about the brain's energy field versus the heart?"

"I only remember they were very different," I answered.

"The electromagnetic field of the brain emits just a few inches beyond the skull," she continued. "The heart's field is 5,000 times more powerful and emits within an 8 to10 foot radius around the body."

"Oh, I see," I said. "The heart determines intention, correct?"

"Yes! The heart is significantly more powerful than the brain in manipulating these fields."

"This means the Universe or electromagnetic field will get behind our choices, right?" I asked. "The ego can choose to suffer or the heart can choose to be free? Wow! Job somehow knew the heart was more powerful, thirty-six hundred years ago and IT was the better choice."

"Exactly," she smiled. "This ancient dream suggests that the ego wants us to believe that negative attention (from God) is better than no attention at all."

"You mean," I said, "that we believe that being judged is our divine inheritance or as some would say evidence of God's presence in our lives?"

Voices

"Yes, divinity is considered the spiritual aspect of being human. Not much unlike grace, divinity is favor that is undeserving. It is regarded as a godly quality and God given."

"Meaning we don't really have to do anything for it?" I asked. "God gives it to us automatically. I have always thought of grace and divinity as being like water to a fish. It is above, below, and to the left and right, invisible to the fish, yet keeping it buoyant."

"If a fish had an ego like we do, it would probably sink," she said smiling. "Water to that fish is analogous to the electromagnetic field for us."

"That's true, isn't it?" I said.

"I hope you see the significance of these comparisons," Rachel said. "Imagine, Job, and by extension humanity, is discerning that hearing the ego's criticism for how we are living our lives is worse than it's (or God's) silence."

"Because," I said, "there is no such thing as a judging God, right?" I paused, taking in the ramifications of this. "It's almost like we are asking for the 'fateful noise' of the ego because we can't handle complete silence." I couldn't believe the depth of these insights—and they were all coming from Job's self-talk.

"It's more that we cannot stand silence because—like Job—when the ego is silent, we are left with the sound of our true voice," she said. "And, our true voice is tied to the heart. We can't do self-deception in the truth."

"This is where the dream gets really interesting," she continued. "For us to live without worry or fear of negative events, or without fear of making a mistake, a promise has to be made."

"What kind of promise?" I asked.

The Astonishing Dream of JOB

"We were supposed to make a promise to feel indebted to the ego and hold it above our heart's wisdom," she answered.

"Was Job able to do that?" I asked.

"That's the point," she answered. "His heart questions this promise, which is why he is suffering. The idea is that if we worship the source of fear which is ego, that this same ego will reward us with moments of fearlessness."

"Seems like a double-edged sword," I said.

"Yes, it is…" Rachel's voice trailed off as she acknowledged an older man, perhaps in his late sixties, walking toward us.

"The gentleman approaching us is Father Bill Ogden," she whispered. "He came here about six months ago and immediately took off his collar and took a leave of absence from the church. He's examining how Job coped with despair."

As he arrived, Rachel introduced us.

"Hello, Father," I said.

"Just call me Bill," he replied, smiling. "Out of uniform means I'm out of character."

"I'll let you two talk while I work on my notes," Rachel said sitting down in the shaded grass.

I shook Rachel's hand and thanked her for her time.

"Bye, Rachel," Father Ogden waved.

"Oh, it's not goodbye," she countered. "I will catch up with you two shortly. I thought you might like some time alone. I get to talk to Father Ogden all the time."

Father Ogden was a tall thin man with black hair, gray streaks at his temples. He looked like he hadn't shaved since he arrived. Right away he began to share his own findings on the topic at hand. He was most interested, he told me, in Job's reaction to despair because it read like a negotiation.

He explained how it was one of the more complicated sections of the dream. Father Ogden felt that these texts would have great spiritual worth to the world.

"As you might imagine, this would be of interest to a priest," he smiled. "Job is questioning the use of guilt. That we may make mistakes and deserve criticism, yes, but Job asks whether our guilt is balanced. Because of exaggerated self-blame and self-punishment we experience a deep sadness."

"So," I said, "he's looking at the emotions that guilt can cause?"

"Yes," Father Ogden replied. "In this instance, he speaks of how fear drains us of our spirit and anger divides us."

"My sense, based upon talking to Zoe and Rachel, is that Job is questioning the pros and cons of suffering. Is that accurate?"

"Yes," he answered. "Job recognizes that personal growth comes from suffering, but he feels that the lack of balance of this kind of suffering can contaminate the soul with anguish. The insight at this point is that at least we have one comfort."

"What is that?" I asked.

"That the ego spares no one."

Hearing this left a sinking feeling in my stomach. "What an incredible and sad truth that since the beginning, we have suffered with the human ego," I thought. Though it is true than none of us can avoid it, hearing someone verbalize it this way took my breath away.

"For the first time in the text," Father Ogden continued, "we see Job questioning his own inner guidance. He is not

The Astonishing Dream of JOB

sure of his stamina or patience, but he realizes that his self-judgments are not going to just stop on their own, and so he searches deeper for help."

I was dumbfounded by the whole conversation. Here we were, speaking about the inner journey of someone who lived thirty-six hundred years ago, and so much of what he discovered was relevant today. That we were privy to a deeper understanding of Job's struggle because we were looking at the Book of Job as an ancient dream interpretation was very humbling.

"What does Job find?" I asked.

"He learns that once we lose the mercy and confidence of our inner voice, we are fated to live in fear of it!"

He paused. "Do you see the significance of this?" he asked.

"Yes," I answered. "We lose compassion for ourselves."

"Absolutely," he replied. "If you fear your emotions, fear will be your experience. More importantly, if you fuel your thoughts with fear you will never trust them again."

Bill went on to say that once we become aware of our inner affliction, we are afraid. This is why so many of us seek guidance, so that we can find peace. He explained that Job's questioning was not so much to argue, but about needing to find an ethical context to explain what he was feeling.

"The dream interpretation offers us a glimpse of Job's philosophy at the time. And it fits our modern day struggle."

"Could you elaborate on that?" I asked.

"Job saw that life is an active struggle between competing forces: what the heart knows and the ego believes. Then (as is the case now), millions of us go through our lives on automatic rather than approach life for the richness it can bring. At the end of the day, many of us would rather be doing something else. Months can go by and all we accomplish is counting our worries at night. Low-lying depression and anxiety is running rampant in our society, so much so that over half the population is suffering."

"That all sounds pretty sad," I said.

"Job's dream is an ancient definition of despair that fits the present," he replied. "It comes with a sense of lost time and a feeling of suffering alone. More people feel this way in our world today than you might imagine. But remember, Job's question throughout his experience was: Are we fated to be afraid of being afraid?"

"So he is challenging that fate?" I asked. "Do we get an answer to this question?"

"Not quite," he replied. "But we do get a better question."

I frowned. "What do you mean?"

"Well," Father Ogden said, "In sharing the bitterness of his soul, Job asks: Are we as vast as the ocean, or merely a whale in a fish bowl?"

"I say … as vast as the ocean," I replied, smiling.

"Of course you would!" he laughed. "That's because you've figured out that freedom is an essential part of being spiritual. Job knows this, too. Again, this is why he is suffering. His challenge, in a world that worships and fears ego, is which is more valid—the heart's truth or the ego's? In this example from the dream text (not the Bible), we see that the heart is."

"So, what is Job feeling as he is weighing the answer to his question?" I asked. "He's having some sleepless nights as he is learning that the ego can frighten us while we sleep by creating terrifying images in our dreams. His soul is trying to suspend the event long enough for Job to have a catharsis, but Job wants the pain to stop."

"The discovered dream translation is very specific at this point," he said. "Job asks: If ego is in our thoughts every morning, and trying us every moment, how long will it go on before we drown in our own emotions?"

"I've often used that metaphor," I said. "When someone is consumed in their emotions, I say they are drowning at the shallow end of the pool. Job seems to have figured that out!"

"Yes," he answered. "But the difference is that Job wants to know what he has done to be haunted in this life forever by fear."

I thought about that for a minute, and then realized that Father Ogden had circled our walk back to Rachel. We were finished and I still had so many questions.

"Well, that didn't take too long," Rachel said, standing up to greet us.

"Did you learn anything new?" Rachel asked.

"Yes," I said. "That examining Job's inner voice offers us some profound guidance."

I was noticing the noise of a passing car when Rachel asked, "Where did Zoe go?"

"She left to meet up with her friends," I said.

"She told me what she did to that inquiring couple you met earlier, sending them away from the synagogue. I think she was a little concerned about what you thought about that," Rachel said.

I laughed. "I might have looked surprised, but it made sense. I didn't have any bad thoughts about it at all."

The truth was that the whole idea that skeptics would attack any new interpretation of an ancient biblical story struck me as ironic. The messages that were being gleaned from these studies would ultimately benefit everyone. Before I could share this thought with Rachel, however, we were distracted by some people walking past.

"You know, I think it's time to do the tourist thing," Rachel said. "You'll want to follow those folks. The woman leading the group gives tours of the surrounding gardens every day."

As we followed three young women to a beautifully manicured garden, I heard the guide say that it was built by members of the Baha'i religion. We walked for several minutes, wandering the garden's paths and enjoying the meticulously designed flower-beds.

"Isn't this a peaceful place?" Rachel asked. I nodded. "Are you going to be in Akko long?" she asked next.

"Only a week," I said. "My friend is meeting the Rabbi at the mosque to discuss the dream interpretation."

"That's right," she said. "Zoe told me. Does your friend have access to portions we haven't seen? We have been so engrossed in examining what we have, and studying our notes, we hadn't considered asking you about your sources."

"Honestly," I said. "I have gotten more from you all today than my friend has shared with me. He's not a very revealing person. How about I promise to stay in touch with you and email what he learned from the Rabbi?"

"That would be great!" Rachel answered giving me her email address.

"I only hope it will be as rich as what I've learned today," I said. "Do you have Father Ogden and Zoe's addresses as well?"

The sun was dropping behind the mountains, but there was still just enough light to appreciate the garden. The sea air held a hint of fish from the nearby pier. It was a wonderful place to end the day.

At the restaurant where Pieta and I had agreed to meet, people were hustling to get a table. I turned the corner and there he was, standing in line. Apparently he had been here a while because he was only second in line to be seated. There had to be thirty people in line behind him.

"Thanks for holding my place," I joked as I slid in beside him. "Have you been here long?"

"Long enough to have an appetite," he said. "So, how did your afternoon go?"

"It was absolutely wonderful and thought-provoking," I said.

I relayed my experience to Pieta, who listened without interruption until I came to the discussion about Job's voices and the content of his self-talk.

"What did everyone say about Job's emotional rant when he realizes that his heart's truth is being challenged?" he asked.

"I think the consensus from everyone was best stated by Father Ogden," I said. "Once we lose the mercy and confidence of our inner voice, we are fated to live in fear of it!"

"Well, we are certainly seeing from Job's reaction that we may have another choice. In his emotional rant we begin to learn about the ground that fear is built on."

"Ground?" I questioned.

Pieta smiled and handed me a translation that was clearly from the Rabbi at the mosque. I shared with him how Zoe had been attending the same conference. Pieta seemed pleased by this as he handed me his notebook. Pieta had written himself a note at the top of the first page: "Can we grow without suffering? Or, if we are at a peak in our lives and we are not truly seen, will we wither before the world?"

"What does this note mean?" I asked.

"The Rabbi gave me this verse from the dream interpretation. It's a reminder that we cannot forget the power of ego. Many of us believe it holds dominion over our self-perception and self-esteem."

"That explains why many of us never reach our full potential," I said, remembering my talk with Father Ogden: vast as the ocean or a whale in a fish bowl.

"Yes," he replied. "The message in this brief passage is that the connection to our ground is built on enormous insecurity. And that this is a place where most of us will stay. It is here that fear grows—without fail."

Over dinner, Pieta and I reveled in conversation about the ancient dream, meeting with the Rabbi, my new friends, and the introduction of Job's inner voices. The questions it stirred in me were exhilarating. It was hard not to be excited after meeting so many wonderfully spiritual people. Pieta assured me that the following day would take us in a wholly different direction.

The Astonishing Dream of JOB

Voices

3

Spiritual Truths

21. Spiritual skepticism: asking why whatever is happening is occurring.

22. We are aware of three inner voices: guidance, condemnation, and synthesis of the two. There is a fourth: the one that rages against the self.

23. Emotions are memories that re-enact our lives.

24. Freedom is an essential aspect of being spiritual.

25. Spiritual confusion: are we born to suffer or to be spiritually free? Truth: we are born to do both.

26. The ego wants us to believe that negative attention (self-judgment) is better than no attention at all—better than silence.

27. Myth: if we worship fear it will reward us with moments of peace in its absence.

28. When we lose the mercy of our inner voice, we are destined to live in fear of it.

29. The soul suspends time or events long enough for us to have a catharsis, while the ego just wants the pain to stop.

30. A ground built on insecurity is fertile ground for fear to grow.

The Astonishing Dream of JOB

4

The Tirade

After dinner, Pieta and I spent the night wandering Akko. With so many tiny little alleyways and very few signs, it was amazing we didn't get lost. Akko is a fascinating town, a melting pot of Muslims and Jews. Pieta wanted to explore our way to where we were staying next rather than use a map. Fortunately for us, Akko is not that big. Walking around until we came to our destination, we ended up standing in front of a house with an open door. Pieta decided to walk in. There were busy sounds coming from a kitchen in the background. Pieta snapped a picture of a clothesline hanging just inside the door.

"I guess every human being in the world still has to do their laundry," Pieta said smiling. "This is the place. These folks are friends of the Rabbi from the mosque."

As we waited for our host, I stepped outside to watch the sun setting on Akko. I found myself staring at the colors. They were beautiful. A Muslim celebration was underway down the street. People were dancing and I could see them carrying a holy object that was being passed around. This night had already been a nice goodbye to the city. As our host showed us our room, I heard Pieta making plans to rent another vehicle for tomorrow's trip. He was discussing where he could obtain supplies, but as usual, he was leaving me out of any decision-making. The meal and the day's excitement had left us both exhausted, so I didn't press too hard to find out any details.

***

The sound of Pieta angrily honking the horn at a local cow that wouldn't move off the road woke me up from my nap. I hadn't slept that well the night before, as the Rabbi's friends only had cots for us to sleep on. I had dozed at the beginning of our trip and barely remembered getting into the car and saying goodbye to our host. I thought it was noon, but it was actually closer to 4 p.m. As I shifted my weight to straighten up, I could feel a spasm forming in my lower back. The pickup truck we had rented was not being kind to me.

At least eight hours had passed since leaving Akko, and I couldn't believe I was capable of sleeping the whole way. Had we driven in the same direction the entire time? I knew Pieta was on another mission, but I didn't know to where or for what. Two days into this journey and I was still without an explanation for Pieta's secrecy. Thank goodness I had met Zoe and Rachel the day before. It felt good to be piecing things together for myself. There was still something he wasn't telling me, but I did not want that to consume my thoughts.

Pieta was so intent on getting to wherever we were going that I couldn't bring myself to disturb his concentration by bringing up more of my conversations from the day before. He was more serious today than he had been at dinner. Just when I thought we might not talk at all that day, he suddenly, without warning, pulled over and told me we needed to talk.

The Tirade

"Do you remember that one of the first spiritual messages of this ancient text was that truth is found in a heart that is convinced of something?" he asked. "Has that been your experience so far? Do you feel that the spiritual truths are resonating for you?"

"That has been my feeling every time," I said, smiling. "I am feeling more and more convinced that Job believed that the human heart is wiser than the ego."

"And you are beginning to agree with him, yes?" he asked.

"Absolutely," I answered. "Aren't you?"

"Yes, yes, of course," he replied. "Every day I want to learn as much as possible about the dream text. But before we can unravel its mystery, we have to solve a problem."

Pieta looked at me, his expression determined. A problem? I anticipated he was on the verge of finally telling me something important. Thus far we had been discussing Job's predicament of internal strife as a physical reaction to an outside event. It was a profound premise and yet easy enough to understand. I knew we were here in Israel to network with others who had heard the same rumors about the dream's discovery. Teachers and students alike were flooding the city of Akko, but now what was this problem to solve?

"You're going to have to explain," I said.

"I know I'm confusing you. Let me explain. I spoke with my mentor in the States yesterday after you went to sleep. He said we still need to find . . . " his voice trailing off.

Pausing for a moment, he said, "I think we should go south to a place called Masada, a small village near Hebron. There are rumors that others like us are gravitating toward locations around the Dead Sea. My mentor suggested that was the direction we needed to go."

The Astonishing Dream of JOB

I was still unclear about the problem we needed to solve, but supportive of Pieta's decision. He told me that the village of Masada was on a huge rock next to the Dead Sea. You could get to the top of it taking one of two paths. It was built and used as a fortress in 103 BC. In 35 BC, Herod the Great took Masada and planned to use it as a hold in case things turned sour for him with Cleopatra. In 66 AD, zealots captured the fortress, which then became a Jewish refuge. Pieta wanted to get to the rock base and possibly camp there if we could.

"The story goes," he said, "that there were 967 people in 70 CE living on the summit of Masada when the Romans tried to capture it. But the Jews decided they would rather die, so ten people were chosen to kill the other 957 men, women, and children and then set fire to the place and commit suicide themselves."

"That's horrible!" I said.

"Yeah," he said. "It turns out they found a woman and child who had hidden from the killing, which is how the story of what happened, is known."

"Unbelievable," I responded. "So what makes you think we might find what we need there?" I asked, still puzzled by our earlier conversation.

"Well," he said, "we used to think that emotions were purely mental expressions generated by the brain. We now know that this is not true—emotions have as much to do with the heart and body as they do with the brain. Said differently, the heart plays an important role in our emotional experience. A lot of locals here think that there was no better display of heart than at Masada in the spring of 73 CE. The spiritual significance, though tragic, may activate our inner compass for what we need to find. Does that make sense?"

The Tirade

I told him it sort of did, and that I would honor his decision to go.

"What are we looking for, exactly?" I asked, unable to control my curiosity any longer.

Pieta hesitated before he answered. "My mentor lacks ... well, you will see soon enough," he said. "Let me just say we are looking for something that pulls all of these spiritual truths together."

I took this to mean there was a missing piece. I wondered if it was a portion of the document itself or another seeker Pieta was hoping to find who had more information.

I had read that there was a lot of salt in the air this close to the Dead Sea, but the air was very dry and carried little, if anything, but dust. I thought to myself that this must be the reason things like the Dead Sea Scrolls could last so long and be so well-preserved. It was this climate. "Better put these on," Pieta said, pulling two pairs of goggles from a bag under the seat and strapping his own set over his eyes. "The wind is picking up."

Thank goodness Pieta planned ahead and had obtained supplies and gear for this trip. He must have gone to the store while I was sleeping. Again, I couldn't believe how much I was sleeping. It wasn't lost on me that he had spoken to his mentor, gotten supplies, and driven for many hours while I was conked out. I wasn't sure if it was just the travel, or the climate, or both, but I had never been so tired. I noticed he had filled the flatbed with sleeping bags, tents, flashlights, and even local snacks. The shift to cooler weather made me appreciative of his compulsion to be prepared. Ahead, as the road curved, all we could see was more and more desert.

The road seemed to go on forever as we drove toward Masada, took a left, and then headed toward a big rock in the distance. It was after 5 p.m. It would be getting dark soon. I was hungry and my stomach was starting to complain. And the further we got into the desert, the more Pietas' statement about needing to find something occupied my thoughts.

Deciding to follow my intuition rather than focus on my frustration, I told Pieta I wanted to turn around and head back toward Hebron. He complied without arguing with me. Once we'd gone about a mile back in the direction we'd come from, I recognized a road and told him to turn onto a dirt path leading up to a hill. He looked at me with a smile as if to imply he trusted my initiative. I told him I remembered seeing this road on a map the day before. In was my belief that this is the way to the Masada fortress.

On the side of the road, near a sign moving in the wind was a vehicle parked with the hood open. There was a man pacing back and forth, waving for us to stop. As we drove up, the burn on his arms and face suggested he had been stranded for a while. I noticed Pieta was trying to feel out the situation.

"No one comes this way, or this far out, unless they are searching for something," he said to me softly. "This may be the connection we've been looking for. Imagine, it was your frustration that brought us here. Or, maybe it really was your inner compass?"

I smiled. "Or maybe I just have a good memory," I said, referring to the map I had studied the day before.

The wind was increasing, so Pieta tried to position our truck so it would shield the front of the man's vehicle. The man looked pleased that we stopped and dropped to one knee as if to catch his breath.

"Looks like you could use some help," Pieta yelled, leaning out the open window of the passenger side of the truck where I was sitting. The man held a scarf over his mouth to shield the blowing sand. He was squinting to protect his eyes.

The Tirade

"Yes!" he yelled above the wind. "I think my alternator died. The damn thing won't even turn over when I try to start it." The man appeared to be in his early fifties and was taller than he looked from a distance. His accent sounded local.

Pieta beckoned for me to get out of the truck and he walked around and met up with us on my side of the truck where we were better shielded from the wind. The man introduced himself as Amit Yosef.

"You're from Israel then?" I asked.

"Yes, I am," he replied. "I teach spiritual studies in Akko. I am here at the Dead Sea seeking information about an archaeological artifact that has been found, a dream interpretation of the Book of Job."

I looked at Pieta, who was smiling with approval. "Turns out we are here for the same reason," I said.

Amit looked at me with excitement. "What do you guys know about it?" he asked. "Have you seen the original?"

Before I could reply, Pieta stepped in. "No, we haven't but I feel we are getting close," he said. "We've been driving for hours hoping to run into a fellow pilgrim. We may have to camp here for the night." He looked expectantly at Amit. "That is, if you don't mind the company?"

"Are you kidding," he said. "I thought I was going to be sleeping in my truck tonight. Especially since the winds have started getting worse. My heart told me someone was going to show up—and here you are."

Pieta assured Amit that we had room in our tent for him. "We only have two sleeping bags, though," he said. "Do you have anything to sleep on?"

"I have some blankets and a foam pad," he answered. "That should suffice, don't you think?"

The Astonishing Dream of JOB

Pieta agreed. While the two of them began a conversation about Amit's journey to Israel and the mystery and controversy around the dream text, I looked around for a place to set up camp that might be out of the wind.

"While you looking for a place to set up," Pieta said, "I'll help Amit with his gear."

"Okay," I sighed. The fatigue of the day—probably lethargy from too much sleep—was setting in.

I convinced Pieta that we should set camp beside a gigantic rock formation. The entire area was full of rocky terrain. They loomed on every side of us, making it feel like we were standing at the bottom of a giant, rocky bowl. I made a mental note to be sure to climb onto it in the morning and take pictures.

Pieta had packed everything imaginable—except jackets. It was getting cooler and the wind was fierce. It got really dark, really fast. There were no other people within miles of where we were. In the distance, there were high-voltage towers. During moments when the wind died down, we could hear the sizzle of electricity.

"This climate is something else," I said. "I think I'm getting dehydrated. I've been so caught up in the journey and sleeping so much that I haven't been drinking enough water."

"Well," Pieta added, "thank goodness the blowing sand didn't blind us from the road, or we would have never found this place."

"Are you guy's researchers?" Amit asked.

"No," I said. "We're spiritual seekers like you." Amit gave me a smile of approval.

"Have you seen the text of this dream?" I asked stooping down to examine the small rocks.

The Tirade

The wind was dying down and in those moments of stillness, I realized we had managed to set up camp along a dry streambed. I found myself looking for round rocks while Amit was talking. I thought they would make great souvenirs to take back home.

"I have accumulated a catalog of notes about the messages so far," he said, leaning toward us. "And I agree with what I've heard—that Job's experience is best understood as an inside experience to an outside event. What I have learned so far is that it is giving us some great insight about how human beings suffer. I see portions of the messages every day in the people I counsel."

"What do you do?" I asked.

"Well," he said. "I teach spiritual studies at a local synagogue, but my interest in this interpretation is how it relates to human stress. From what I can tell, as we experience feelings of anger, frustration, anxiety, and insecurity, our heart vibrates erratically. These vibrations are then sent to the emotional centers in the brain as stress. Speaking from my own experience with it, these negative vibrations can block our ability to think clearly."

"Isn't there strong evidence," I asked, "that heart disease is significantly increased in those people who experience these kinds of negative emotions?"

"Absolutely," Amit replied. "I think most medical folks would agree with you on that."

"What is important, though," he continued, "is that heart-felt emotion, like love, gratitude, appreciation, and compassion, all produce an opposite vibration or effect. This means our heart and body responds to positive emotions as well."

Pieta and I were both tired, but Pieta asked him to continue.

The Astonishing Dream of JOB

"Job's emotional rant is a wonderful example of losing clarity and regaining it because of compassion—or self-love," Amit said.

This was exactly what Pieta had asked me about earlier, Job's emotional tirade about what was happening to him. The probability of meeting Amit and having this conversation gave me goose bumps. I could tell that Pieta was pleased. Maybe my heart did guide us here.

"What are your thoughts about Job's emotional meltdown?" Pieta asked.

I looked at Amit's face as he contemplated his answer and it dawned on me that we are at the Dead Sea, an area of the world that is over 1,300 feet below sea level. Considered one of the lowest areas in the world, the Dead Sea is so saline rich that it's six times saltier than the ocean! Nothing can live in its waters. Fish that accidentally swim into the Dead Sea from one of the several freshwater streams that feed it are killed instantly. Because of the extremely high concentration of mineral salts, the water's density is higher than that of fresh water. I remembered reading a brochure in Akko that explained how tourists like floating in the Dead Sea because they are more buoyant. I imagined them bobbing up and down like a cork. As Amit began to speak, I was lost in thoughts of how soothing floating would feel to my back after the long drive.

"The first portion of the text reminds us that we falsely believe we are no match for the ego or that it cannot be argued with," Amit was saying. The probability of winning such an argument, the text says, is one in one thousand."

"Wait," I said. "The dream provides us with a statistic?"

"Yes," he continued. "We learn that the ego's power comes from its awareness and manipulation of the longing within the human heart. Using this longing against us, it can play on our insecurities."

The Tirade

"The longing you speak of," Pieta asked, "is the dreams of our imagination and our passion to pursue them?"

"Absolutely," Amit replied. "The text points out that the ego hides our dreams, as if under a seal. This means they stay hidden from our awareness."

"What is the implication of that?" I asked.

The wind had settled and I was better able to observe Amit. He had black, tangled hair, a square chin, and a tall stature. His whole demeanor was engaging and animated. Like most of the people we had met along our quest, Amit was well-educated and determined. It was easy to forget my fatigue and get lost in his explanations. "Job's message as a dream is clear," he answered. "The ego alone creates and controls the waves of our emotions. It is responsible for our highs and lows, can bring us to tears, and fosters the angst for us to question ourselves."

"I still need some clarification about the tirade," Pieta remarked. "What did Job say to the ego about its interference?"

"That's a great question," Amit answered. "My understanding is that Job is confused about the purpose and function of the human ego. The text indicates that if he could see ego, he would not recognize it. But at the same time, if he didn't have its judgments, he would be confused about what to do next. When the ego initially evaluates him, he takes it as the absolute truth. Few ever ask why such judgments are necessary, but he did."

"That is amazing," I said. "We dislike the judgment but conversely feel lost without it."

Amit laughed. "I think this gets back to being alone with the sound of our own voice. Few of us can be compassionate to ourselves in those moments," he replied.

The Astonishing Dream of JOB

"Certainly, no one can doubt the influence of ego in their world," I said. "The ego's chatter can be overwhelming."

"Because we do not believe the ego will respond to our heart's longing," Amit continued. "Our spirit is not allowed to rest. And this alone begins our battle with resentment."

"This is an example of the injustice Pieta told me about," I said, looking at Pieta for reinforcement. "That is exactly my feeling," Pieta confirmed. "It seems if we are strong in a given moment, the ego is stronger. If we expect to be treated as we treat others, none of us will dare acknowledge this expectation. If we try to justify this desire, then somehow our own words are used against us."

"This is the theme," Amit continued. "Because we have so much difficulty knowing the differences between our inner voices, the text says that even if our soul knows the distinction, we can still be exhausted by life. Job's rant about this is specific."

"What does he say?" I asked.

"If this life is destined to feel wrong," he answered, "then the ego is responsible for these feelings . . . period. The dream interpretation is clear about what the heart knows: we are to have (1) a life full of possibilities, and (2) a spirit that is rewarded. If this potential is not part of the human condition, and all we are left with is ego judgment, then life is tormented with sadness."

Pieta remarked, "I understand this passage to mean that we are destined to fear our accomplishments because we believe they will not be enough to satisfy the ego."

"But," I added, "We all labor even harder to be better."

Amit paused for a moment and I remembered my early conversations in Akko. I stopped to take in the magnificent experience of the backdrop of Masada. Pieta was right—it was moving to be here. What an amazing story, Jewish rebels

The Tirade

making a last stand at the apex of this large fortress atop a mountain cliff, and the depth of their self-sacrifice; was moving to say the least. Since we'd left the States I'd had the sensation that something was guiding us. Has it been our hearts? The light from our lantern made shadows on the rocks. I noticed the redness of Amit's sunburn as he continued.

"The deep message in this portion of the dream is this: If we can remove the ego's judgment from our lives, fear goes with it. Life's deepest answers cannot be discovered if we are afraid," he said.

Pieta smiled. "This means having a full life and experiencing spiritual maturity is possible if we are simply allowed to be who were really are," he replied.

"Exactly!" Amit responded. "Our heart's conviction to being true to itself is separate from the ego's demand to serve it."

As our conversation drifted away from the text I felt it was an opportunity to ask Amit about his time in Akko. Pieta had stretched out on his sleeping bag by that point and Amit was searching for something to drink.

"Have you been in Akko teaching long?" I asked.

"I moved there in December of 2008," he said. "I had heard wonderful things about the city's history and felt the tensions had quieted down by then."

"What tensions?" I asked.

"There was a riot in early October 2008 because some idiot drove his car through a Jewish neighborhood on Yom Kippur. Fortunately, the violence only lasted a few days."

"I didn't hear about that," I said. "Most of us in the States are aware of how fragile Jewish-Arab relations are, but we don't hear about the day-to-day violence."

"Well," he continued. "It wasn't anywhere near as bad as what happened in October 2000. The Israeli police shot dead twelve people, all Arabs, and a visitor from the West Bank."

"Was anyone killed in 2008?" I asked.

"No," he answered. "The Jewish people in the neighborhood forced the car to stop, pulled the driver out, and beat him up. News of the beating spread like wildfire across Akko. By the time the news had traveled from the mosques, Arabs were talking about avenging what by then had been exaggerated to two Arabs having been murdered by Jews."

"We are just crazy," Pieta said, "when fear and prejudice takes over like that."

"Yes," Amit continued. "Hundreds took to the streets, mostly young people, smashing shop windows, shattering car windows, slashing tires, and torching vehicles. It was pretty scary."

"Does any portion of Job's tirade give us advice about this?" I asked, circling back around to the text.

"I wondered if we were done for the evening," Amit smiled. "It turns out that there is some clarity in his emotional speech."

"Enlighten us," Pieta said.

"Well," Amit answered. "The text teaches that because the soul can be exhausted by our lives, the solution is to let go of the prejudice that wears it down. As these riots suggest, and as Job's injustice implies, negative self-talk will have a lasting and bitter effect on the soul."

"Does the ego have any sense of time?" I asked.

"My feeling about this," he answered, "is that the ego only knows its history. Time does not pass at all like it does for us. In fact, it is stuck in the past."

The Tirade

"It creates our sense of self one moment," Pieta replied. "It can even give us the sensation of feeling whole, and then just as quickly condemn us for who we are. It moves in the dimension of fear, not time."

"I love what the interpretation says about this," Amit continued. "It says that the universe provides us a physical body for the inner self, which makes us both strong and resilient. Then we were animated with a compassionate disposition to provide a sanctuary for our spirit."

"That is so beautiful," I said.

"Although this predisposition is hidden in the beginning, it is known in the heart and it can be remembered. If we could all just know that we are in this suffering experiment together, we would live in a different world."

"And for goodness sakes," added Pieta. "If we have this all wrong then at least make our suffering useful and cleansing. Don't allow our pride to make us a victim."

"Yes," Amit said. "Many of us ask why we were even born, if pre-judgments are to keep our personal truths and gifts invisible. This wonderful dream interpretation allows us to ponder the concerns of our predicament. Those who do not are destined to go into the unconscious with their suffering, where they will sit with it forever. What is left is confusion and fear."

As the conversation came to a close, Amit explained that the Arab community leaders issued an apology in 2008 for the violation of the Jewish holy day. The Arab driver went on television in Jerusalem and said he had not intended any provocation but had made a terrible error of judgment. Because it was very late at night, he explained, he thought no one would notice his car driving into the Jewish neighborhood where he lived.

The Astonishing Dream of JOB

"In light of the history of Israeli-Arab conflict and day-to-day tensions," Amit said, "particularly in mixed cities like Akko, rioting there is no surprise. All it takes is something like this to set the two sides against the other."

Like so much of our journey, the conversation with Amit was enlightening and affirming. As the evening ended, we knew that the following day would hold another exciting adventure. Meanwhile, we had to help Amit repair his vehicle. Fortunately, Pieta had every tool imaginable in the truck.

***

It was shortly after dawn; we ate breakfast and worked on Amit's truck until we had it running. Then we grabbed our canteens and headed for the highest peak near our campsite. From there we had an excellent view of the surrounding valley. On the way back down I snapped several photos of the Dead Sea. Though Amit's truck was barely functional, he insisted that he be allowed to lead us back to town.

It felt good to be heading back to modern conveniences, though the evening be-fore had been enlightening. As Pieta guided the truck back onto the main route behind Amit, I had all but forgotten the stress I was feeling the day before. Pieta would tell me soon enough what he was searching for. For now, my head was spinning from the accumulation of things we'd learned so far. As always, I was left with the overwhelming sense that amazing things awaited us, and I couldn't wait to see what was going to come next.

The Tirade

4

Spiritual Truths

31. We falsely believe that the ego cannot be negotiated with.

32. The ego's power comes from its manipulation of our longing.

33. Though we dislike the ego's judgment, we can become confused without it.

34. An ego asleep (unconscious) cannot fix our heart's longing. Because the spirit never rests, this creates a cycle of inner resentment.

35. The heart has two certainties: (1) we have a life full of possibilities, and (2) we are a spirit that is free and joyful.

36. If we remove the ego's judgment from our lives, fear goes with it.

37. Our heart's conviction is to be true to itself while the ego's conviction is for us to serve it.

38. Because the soul can be exhausted by our choices, we must let go of the prejudices that wear it down.

39. Human beings are strong and resilient, have a compassionate disposition and their soul's having bodily form, provides refuge for the human spirit.

40. Although the sacred relationship between body and soul is hidden in the beginning, it is known in the heart and can be remembered.

The Astonishing Dream of JOB

5

I Will Ask

The experience out in the desert with Pieta and Amit made me think of many instances in the Bible where individuals went into the wilderness seeking answers. Many would come out of those experiences having let go of old perceptions and adopted new ones. Jesus himself went many times into the desert. At one point he spent forty days and forty nights fasting, praying, and most important, listening to God. Like Job, he was seeking silence from his inner voice. I wondered if this was the actual voice of God—silence? I figured out that Pieta had wanted to go to Masada for a metaphorical fast—to let go of the personal ego, getting all of the ideas out of his head that were clamoring for attention. It seemed to have worked because I found him to be much calmer the following day.

With all the information I'd gathered so far, I'd come to a few conclusions of my own. Someone in history, possibly in the twelfth century, considered the Book of Job an internal reaction to an outside event. That person wrote a text that interpreted Job's experience as a dream. The text was later stolen and disappeared until its recent discovery. The author remains unknown.

The Astonishing Dream of JOB

After our overnight in the desert, we traveled toward the east coast of Israel to the town of Be'er Sheva. It was my hope that we could speak to local authorities there about what they knew of this theft that would have happened some seven hundred years ago.

"So far Job's experience is showing us that human feelings have validity," I said. "Would you agree?"

"Not only are they valid," Pieta answered. "Our perceptions are clearer when coming from the heart. The challenge as human beings is to figure out if we can communicate with the ego and, if so, whether it responds to our communication."

"So many people confuse their heart and their ego," I replied. "How can we tell what aspect of the self we are talking to, and where the answers are coming from?"

"It is best understood as past versus present," Pieta said. "Ego of the past is formed at a very young age and only knows these early programs. The ego does not age as we age, until something happens to wake it up. In fact, it keeps us in the past reenacting experiences from when it was formed."

The route we were traveling was a curvy, two-lane highway, and most of the time there were no signs warning us of the next steep turn in the road. As we weaved ourselves along the highway, I was pondering the difference between an ego asleep and an ego awake. This was not a distinction I had learned in college, nor one the lay public hears about. As much as I would have liked to have been lost in thought, however, I found myself wondering if there might be a better route, as the curves seemed to be doubling our travel time.

"Wake it up?" I finally asked. "Do you mean that the ego is stuck in the past until it is provoked into the present?"

I Will Ask

"Yes," Pieta answered. "A reenactment gets its energy from an emotion that is coming from the past. It is a biochemical memory before it becomes a déjà vu experience. A reaction is a feeling that comes from the immediate moment. An ego responding to the present moment is doing so because something woke it up, usually adversity. Growth happens because the ego is working in concert with the heart. An ego asleep has not developed this relationship."

"An ego asleep is child-like then," I said. "Emoting in a given moment, it is lost to its fears. Job knew this?"

"Yes," Pieta answered. "Psychology defines ego as reenactments of emotions and earlier conditioning, when in truth this same ego can be awakened—to feel. Job's storm was a wake-up moment."

"This is huge," I said. "We've made a science out of studying the abnormalities of a developing ego, while understanding the experience spiritually can be the restoration—to normal. This doesn't exist in any textbook I've ever read. Incredible!"

"You've got it," Pieta continued. "And, the culture at large is not using adversity as an opportunity for this restoration. Instead, most are stuck in their victimization and staying unconscious."

"Yes, but awakening requires a level of spiritual maturity that is lacking," I said.

"It does," Pieta answered. "And, it supports your metaphor. Most people are drowning in the shallow end of the pool. Few can step back far enough to see that their fears are unwarranted. In truth, objectivity is required to allow for an ethical or a heartfelt view of the self."

It had been over two hours since we left Masada for Be'er Sheva, and while we were engaged in conversation the whole way, we missed very little scenery as it was all desert.

The Astonishing Dream of JOB

A sudden composure washed over Pieta as a sign ahead indicated that we were fifteen minutes from our destination.

Be'er Sheva is an ancient biblical city about one and a half hours from Jerusalem. It is the site where Abraham planted the tamarisk tree and dug a 210-foot-deep well. It is said that he once sent a servant here to find a bride for Isaac. Be'er Sheva is located on the southern border of Solomon's kingdom.

Once we arrived, I left Pieta with the truck, bartering for a parking space. Be'er Sheva is a desert city and very spread out, even by Israeli standards. There isn't much of a downtown, except for a few streets where we were standing. The market is uncovered and the afternoon desert sun was not sparing us because we were tourists. Surprisingly, the market itself was very ordinary. The Bedouin part, or desert-dwelling nomads, were very few. They were at the edge of the market selling traditional carpets and coffee, spices, and galabiya which is a robe the Bedouin men wear. Entering Bedouin Market, my attention was suddenly drawn to several loud thumps from behind. As I turned around, I saw a large semi-truck barreling toward the market and then bounce over a sand ravine.

The vehicle went slightly airborne as everyone watched in horror. The truck hit the back of a pick-up and a concession stand before landing on its side. During the crash, onlookers were scattering to get out of the way. I stood frozen in disbelief.

As the chaos settled, a beautiful woman rushed over to assist the driver of the truck. He appeared to be local but spoke in both Hebrew and English. My Hebrew was not good enough to understand everything that was being said, but the woman's translations helped. I moved closer so I could hear what she was saying. "Did you say you feel like you are having a heart attack?" she repeatedly asked in English. I could tell from her accent that she was Israeli. I heard someone behind me say that emergency personnel had been notified but, for the moment, this woman was managing the scene on her own. The elderly man she was assisting was bleeding from his nose.

"It was my fault," he said loudly. "I lost control in the ravine."

I approached slowly, careful not to interfere. "Is he okay?" I asked.

Natalie responded without looking up. "He said he was coming through Be'er Sheva to shave time off of his route," she said. "As he entered town, he felt a pain in his chest, and before he realized it, he hit the ravine next to the road, jackknifed, and lost control of the vehicle."

The cab of the truck was in the ravine, resting on one set of wheels and the man was partially spilling out of his seat sideways. The door was open and a sheet of broken glass, and perhaps a trapped leg, hindered the man from being able to be set free from the cab. There was gasoline spilling out from some hidden leak and the smell was every-where. A crowd of Israeli bystanders had gathered around, smoking nervously. "Smoking? How crazy," I thought. Maybe it was a lapse of concern for herself, or just a sense of responsibility, but Natalie's take-charge attitude impressed me. Like so many of the people I had met since we arrived in Israel, Natalie assisted this man with such compassion and care. I was worried about the gasoline. Fire trucks and emergency personnel were finally arriving, and blaring sirens were causing the people to scatter.

I helped Natalie encourage the locals to extinguish their cigarettes while an Israeli medic rushed to prepare an IV. A team of bystanders and firemen peeled the windshield glass away, as the medic inserted the IV. For some reason, maybe bad preparation, the IV was not flowing. This meant the

The Astonishing Dream of JOB

medics had to take turns holding it and squeezing the fluid into the poor man's arm.

After securing a backboard, putting on a neck brace, and beginning to ease the man out of his truck, the ambulance showed up. When everyone was booted off the scene, Natalie turned toward me, looking relieved.

"Are you a nurse?" I asked.

"No," she answered. "But I'm pretty sure the guy will be fine. He looks like he might have a head trauma, but at least he didn't go into shock."

She introduced herself as Natalie Kirvat, born in the countryside of Israel to horse-ranching parents. Because Israeli women are required to serve in the military, she had learned a little medical training in the service.

"He's lucky," I said.

"I don't think he was bleeding heavily, or had any life-threatening injuries," she said.

"I just got here," I said. "Heck of a way to begin a visit."

Natalie was an archeologist studying at a nearby university. As she was telling me about her classes, Pieta approached, seemingly having secured the truck. Unscathed by the excitement around the accident, he introduced himself to Natalie.

"We could probably use the help of an archeologist," Pieta said reaching out to shake her hand. "My friend and I are here seeking . . . "

"Let me guess," she interrupted. "You are looking for the dream text of the Job story?"

"Is it obvious?" I asked, smiling.

I Will Ask

"Let's just say we are getting a lot of foreigners here," she replied. "And most are seeking to answer spiritual questions about human suffering."

"Do you know anything about it?" Pieta asked eagerly. "About the text, I mean."

She smiled. "Turns out me and a couple of colleagues and I have recently learned something new about the find." I thought Pieta was going to jump out of his shoes with excitement.

"One of our colleagues," Natalie continued, "was involved in the discovery of a cemetery dating to the late Bronze Age 1550-1200 BCE near the Persian Garden, just north of Akko."

"What did they find there?" I asked.

"Well, the interesting thing about archaeology," she said, "is that we often uncover the good that men do, as well as the bad. And, these secrets are always buried with their bones."

"How many graves were there?" Pieta asked. "And when was this dig?"

"It was in 1971," she said. "All together there were five graves, and the skeletal remains suggested nine individuals. The problem was that the bodies were in such poor condition it was impossible to determine familial ties or cause of death."

"Interesting," I said, marveling over the fact that people like Natalie sifted through dead remains for a living. "So were they able to find anything out?"

"Their history and activity was reconstructed from what was found buried with the bones," she said.

As we listened, I noticed that Pieta was totally captivated by Natalie as she unraveled the story about the mysterious

The Astonishing Dream of JOB

gravesite. It was as if he knew that this information was going to move us forward on our quest.

"This is fascinating," I said.

"It turns out," she continued, "that the deceased were buried with an uncharacteristically abundant amount of specialized goods. There was a large quantity of Late Cypriot Bronze Age ceramic imports, specifically rare Mycenaean pottery, copper and bronze weapons, tools, and implements."

"Could you tell who they were from their possessions?" Pieta asked.

"Well, the weapons may represent the personal possessions of warriors," she said. "They also recovered a fine bronze Egyptian mirror and a number of strange items, some pottery that was not consistent with 1336 BC, the time in question. And some of the items and their functions eluded interpretation altogether. The researchers weren't sure who these people were initially."

Pieta shifted his weight impatiently, clearly having difficulty as Natalie's story unfolded. He wanted it to tie in with the dream text more quickly.

"I'm not sure how this excavation relates to our quest for Job's text," he finally said.

Natalie smiled. "Be patient," she said. "It gets better, and it will eventually make sense. Have you ever heard of the Amarna Letters?" she asked.

I didn't give Pieta a chance to answer. "I never have," I said. "What are they?"

"The Amarna Letters are an archive of correspondence on clay tablets, mostly diplomatic, between the Egyptian administration and its representatives in Canaan and Amurru during the New Kingdom 1550-1070 BC. They were found

I Will Ask

in Upper Egypt at Amarna, and are an unusual find in Egyptological research because they're mostly written in Akkadian cuneiform, the writing system of ancient Mesopotamia, not ancient Egypt."

I found myself captivated by Natalie's storytelling. She was deeply intelligent and had a wealth of knowledge about this area of the world and its history. But how all this related to our journey was still unclear. I could tell that Pieta was eager to hear more but was biting his tongue.

"My colleagues carbon dated these bodies and figured out they were from the time these tablets were written. They also found a parallel in Amarna Letter 7 where Burnaburiash II writes to Akhenaten, speaking of the role of someone named Biryawaza, who was Egypt's representative in Upi—Egypt at the time. "Burnaburiash accused Biryawaza of robbing a caravan belonging to a merchant in his employ. It seems not only had the caravans been robbed, but Burnaburiash's merchants were murdered and their silver stolen. Burnaburiash clearly identified Zatatna, king of Akko, as the perpetrator of this robbery and murder."

"So," I thought. "Burnaburiash was saying that Zatatna, King of Akko, hired Biryawaza to rob the caravan. Why would an Israeli king employ someone to do that?"

Natalie was suggesting that all of this somehow tied to our search for the dream text, but I still wasn't making any clear connections.

"Do we have evidence that this is true?" I asked.

"It turns out that the evidence rested with the bones of the nine individuals," Natalie said. "They were not warriors but merchants with members of their families, robbed and murdered by Zatatna and his co-conspirators."

"How can you be sure?" Pieta asked.

The Astonishing Dream of JOB

"First, the small cemetery is only two-and-a-half kilometers south of Akko, and there is no other settlement nearby. Second, it is an unusual and odd place for a burial ground. And finally, despite the wealth buried with the bodies and the careful arrangement of the objects in the grave, the graves themselves were poorly and hastily dug pits in the sand."

"Archeology is a fascinating field," I said. "The fact that you can learn all of this from a gravesite is unbelievable."

Natalie nodded. "The bodies had already begun to decompose before they were buried in the sand pits, suggesting that they were exposed to the elements for a long time before they were buried."

"So the bodies were moved from where the murder originally took place?" Pieta asked.

"Exactly," she replied. "Now, to the dream text you are so interested in."

I could feel my heart begin to race as Natalie readied herself to fill in the blanks of our search. Pieta sighed, seemingly relieving the tension of his impatience.

"As I mentioned, there were some items at the gravesite that resisted interpretation, and there was pottery that was out-of-date for the find," she said.

Pieta and I both nodded.

"Well," she replied. "There was a red clay ceramic pot that dated to the Mamluke period, from the mid-twelfth to the early fifteenth centuries. Akko was ruined by the Mamlukes in 1291 and then it was abandoned. The city's harbor was destroyed and blocked to prevent the return of the Christians after the Crusades."

"Don't tell me they found something in this clay pot," I said excitedly.

I Will Ask

Natalie smiled. "Yes they did. Lining the inside wall of the pot was a wax substance over a parchment. The writing was Arabic and barely legible. My colleagues recognized it as referring to the book of Job, but it was not another version like the four found in the 1950s."

Natalie went on to explain that four partial translations of the Book of Job were discovered in 1956 at Qumran in Egypt. The four fragments were portions of one of the two translations, or Targums, of the original Hebrew of Job into Aramaic, the predominant language of Judea after the Babylonian Exile. The texts discovered in Qumran were the earliest Targum of a biblical book.

"This is incredible," Pieta said excitedly hearing this new information. "We now have stronger evidence about the origin of the text that translates the Book of Job as a dream. So it is not a manuscript from biblical times, but rather something that was written in the twelfth century?"

"It seems so," Natalie answered. "And, yes it was the interpreter's rendition of Job's experience. We are just now learning it is a dream interpretation. We are not sure how it ended up in this particular site. A logical answer would be that it was stolen and buried there."

"Do you have any sense of the author and why he took this approach to a controversial biblical story?' he asked.

"Whoever the author was, he or she was very much aware of the wisdom teachings being discussed in the twelfth and thirteenth centuries," she said. "And clearly, they believed in the prophetic nature of dreams."

"Are you aware of the messages," I asked, "coming from the dream text we've been searching?"

"Yes, I am," she said. "Like you, I have my sources. My interest in this document came out of its take on spiritual freedom. When I heard that the interpretation says that the ego dwells in a place of perfection and we are unable to comprehend its intent or even know it at all, that bothered me. To suggest that the ego is larger than our ground, and deeper than our feelings, upset me deeply. This would mean that the ego determines perfection when, in truth, it points out our imperfections. No wonder humans live with such dissatisfaction about themselves."

"So you want to understand and learn more about the dream text?" I asked.

"Yes," she said, smiling. "I, too, am compelled to find this document and bring its meaning to the spiritual community."

Pieta had been turning over in his mind the significance of what Natalie was saying. He had a look of affirmation on his face when he finally spoke.

"My source on this text has told me that when human beings feel good about themselves," he said, "they believe they exist to be free and without controls. Not having this freedom to be is the source of their suffering."

"Ironically, fear is the control," she replied. "And if we do not understand these fears they harden our heart, yes?" Natalie asked.

"Yes, I think Job knew this," he answered. "Human beings know there is wisdom in the heart. That the heart knows more than the ego knows. This is the reason he is so adamant with his questions. Job says: 'I will ask and you will answer.' He knows that fear hardens the heart ... not wisdom."

"Is it not true," Natalie continued, "that insights from our own inner compass inform us of this? We somehow know that some higher authority than ego is responsible for our guidance. The heart has its own intelligence and is connected to the soul and spirit of who we are?"

I Will Ask

"Yes, the heart is wise and strong," Pieta continued. "It counsels and understands. This twelfth-century dream text suggests that if we use the heart to turn against ourselves, no one can repair the damage. If a bitter heart takes away our voice, no one can help us speak. If the heart isn't allowed to self-express, we ultimately will dry up."

"So, the heart's intelligence can override the ego, yes?" I asked.

"Correct," answered Pieta. "Self-deception is the trick of the ego. In our hearts, we cannot deceive ourselves. The ego's ultimate deception is that it gets us to view it as a person. We give IT an identity. That is the ego's secret."

"Please continue," Natalie said. "This is a curious distinction."

"We are deceived when we consider 'I' and 'me' as the real self." Pieta continued. "These are the names of the ego. Or, we are deceived when we give the ego its own separate identity and internalize it as shadow or our less visible side."

"If I understand you correctly," she said, "the author of this interpretation wants us to value our feelings."

"Absolutely," Pieta answered. "Or control our feeling reactions long enough to get a reading on the immediate experience we are in. Feeling does not wound the soul, only the ego can do that."

"I still struggle with whether the ego is the enemy when we are trying to be our true selves," I said. "Is it?"

"My mentor tells me that the ego will protect the emotional if it has been awakened to the present," Pieta replied. "It will do this because truth is in the immediate moment, not the past. In fact, there are only two things that the heart fears when it reveals itself."

"Two?" Natalie said with a confused reading on her face. "The heart only fears two things?"

"Yes," Pieta answered. "According to our mysterious twelfth-century author, we are afraid, one, that once love is gone it will be lost forever and, two, without it, fear will become all consuming."

"Wow!" I said. "The absence of love is the dimension of fear, right?"

"Exactly!" Pieta said. We both glanced at Natalie in that moment, who was wiping tears from her eyes. Clearly, our conversation was touching on something she identified with.

"Not to worry dear, this text is reinforcing something many of us have long known—that love is a place," Pieta said.

"Why do you think we are still struggling with this after centuries of wars and indifference toward each other?" she asked.

"Simply put," he said, "religion tells us that we were conceived in the beginning as a mistake. This egoic and incredible judgment plagues the planet."

"What does such a fate leave us with?" I asked.

"Well, Pieta responded. "It suggests that the collective ego has assigned us the task of achieving perfection."

"Uh," I said. "That's not going to happen."

"Perfection in this context," he continues, "is us being the most authentic version of ourselves that we can be. Our daily practice is to provide ourselves with a spiritual time-out or rest from the ego to imagine our dreams. A broken spirit and a soul stripped of its worth isn't going to have much of an imagination, let alone the energy to pursue it."

I Will Ask

"I have had that feeling," Natalie added. "The one where you feel detached from the source and your spirit is empty. What follows is numbness. It is a lonely and sad place."

"Who or what is going to protect us in these moments?" I asked. "I mean, spiritually, how do we cope with a spirit that has been defeated?"

"The interpretation suggests that when we experience a 'spiritual death' we will come out the other side reborn. All the days, months, and years we are under attack by the ego are made tolerable because of the possibility of that transformation. We cope in the interim by being as ethical and compassionate toward the self as we can be."

"Compassion allows us to be spiritually reborn multiple times?" Natalie asked.

"Yes," I answered. "This is the realm of the soul's intent, is it not? The soul orchestrates us through the maze of these judgments, gets us to see what we need to see to initiate a transition, and requires compassion for the self, which ultimately allows a transformation to happen."

"It is important to see that in this context the ego creates the angst that makes us question our will to be," Pieta explained. "Job's decision: 'I will ask . . . ' is the inheritance and gift of what it means to be human. If we didn't ask questions or if we believed we had all the answers, human beings wouldn't have evolved spiritually at all."

Our discussion was energizing and enriching. I could tell that Pieta was pleased, as he apologized to Natalie for his earlier impatience. Thanking her repeatedly, Pieta made sure to express his gratitude for her contribution to our journey. It was 6 p.m. If we were going to explore Be'er Sheva and get to bed at a reasonable hour, we needed to say our farewells to Natalie. She wished us well and gave us the name of a reputable inn nearby, and asked if it was okay to have one of her contacts call us in the morning. We said yes

The Astonishing Dream of JOB

and Pieta gave her his cell phone number. Our plan was to get an early start in the morning and head toward Gaza.

First we visited the Negev Brigade Memorial, located in the northern-most area of the Negev, Israel's desert. It was simply a series of concrete structures, but the view was more revealing than interesting.

Pieta continued to reflect about the evening's conversation. "This day has turned out to bring more than I could have imagined," he said. "Had you not walked over to Natalie, we may have never gotten the information about the text and its origin."

I couldn't help but think about the synchronicity of today's events. In fact, had Natalie not been captured by the circumstances, I wouldn't have had the opportunity to meet her at all. Like so many of our experiences, it seemed as if something was guiding us.

Over the course of our conversation, Pieta explained how much he valued our friendship and how he had few people in his life he could share such an experience with. I pondered about how our trek to Israel came about. Though I hadn't known what to expect, I agreed that our time together was proving to be better than either of us could have wished for.

As we continued, we came across local musicians playing instruments in a twenty-foot-tall dome. The structure reverberated incredibly well and invented an unlikely place for an outside display of guitar playing. The split in the dome was aligned with lines in the floor and made a massive but beautiful sundial.

"You know," I said smiling. "It would be nice if you would share with me what it is exactly we're searching for. There's a lot you're not telling me."

"I know, I know," Pieta said. "You have been very patient with me."

I Will Ask

"You have always been so good at keeping me in suspense or baiting me to figure things out on my own," I said. "But, I'm truly stumped this time."

We laughed about the nature of our relationship and found some relief in the levity. Pieta promised that my questions would be answered soon.

"It will all make sense shortly," Pieta said. "Meanwhile, we're both growing spiritually from the experience, yes?"

"Absolutely," I replied.

"Trust me, my friend," Pieta continued. "It may not seem like it at times but, we are a team. I may make the plans and confer with my mentor in the States, but you're much better at approaching the locals."

"That certainly seems to be our pattern, and I am a little more personable than you," I joked.

"Exactly," he laughed. "Today's experience is a wonderful example of that. It's because of you that some of these pieces are coming together."

It felt good to laugh and hear Pieta's reassurance about my contribution to our quest. We ended the evening with a visit to the British World War I Military Cemetery. We were particularly touched by the introspective life quotes on the headstones.

The day had been full of so much introspection and reflection. Now that we had some important pieces to our puzzle, the quest to Gaza tomorrow was certain to gain momentum.

The Astonishing Dream of JOB

I Will Ask

5
Spiritual Truths

41. The heart's intelligence is connected to the soul and spirit of who we are; working together the three can guide the ego.

42. Self-deception is the norm for ego, but the heart is unable to deceive itself.

43. The ego's ultimate deception is to present itself as who we are (I or ME) and get us to serve it.

44. The heart only has two fears: (1) that once love is gone it will be lost forever and (2) without love, the heart's fears will become all consuming.

45. Our daily practice is to provide ourselves a spiritual time-out from the ego and time to imagine our dreams.

46. A broken spirit and a soul stripped of its worth isn't going to have an imagination, let alone the energy to pursue it.

47. When we experience a "spiritual death" this is ego waking up.

48. All the days, months, and years we are under attack by the ego are made tolerable because of the possibility for spiritual transformation.

49. The soul's intent is to get us through the maze of our ego judgments, help us see what we need to see, give us the compassion to tolerate the

experience, and make us a witness of our own transformation.

50. Irony: the ego creates the angst that makes us question our will to be and, without this angst we would not move spiritually.

6

The Companion

The day started strangely, with a cell phone call to Pieta at 8:30 a.m. over breakfast at a local café in Gaza City. Pieta and I had driven forty-five kilometers from Be'er Sheva and had left early like we planned. We were expecting a phone call, so when Pieta's phone rang I just assumed it was Natalie's contact.

I could overhear the voice on the other end of the line—a gruff male voice. When Pieta hung up, he informed me that it was not who we thought it was, but rather that Natalie's contact had passed our information along to someone else entirely. We'd been instructed to be at a certain place in a half-hour—and the man, whoever he was, would not wait. Pieta made a quick phone call to his friend at the Ramhal Synagogue in Akko to discuss what was unfolding. I wondered if there were any inherent risks in meeting this person—even more of a complete stranger than Natalie's contact. After all, we were in Gaza and the situation here was not always predictable. But together we decided this meeting presented a rare opportunity not to be missed. We paid the waitress and hailed a taxi.

The Astonishing Dream of JOB

The city of Gaza is the principal city in the Gaza Strip, and is under the control of the Palestinian Authority, who took it over from Israel after the 1993 Oslo Accords. Gaza is a sought-after territory because of its location between Asia and Africa, its fertile land, and its value as a seaport.

Gaza-based militant groups have been involved in countless rocket attacks on Israel, and the kidnapping of soldiers as recently as two years before our journey. Our taxi driver informed us that he was in fact one of these militant fighters, but was quick to add that he would never let his son fire a gun. He said he fights only to make a better future for his family.

Our taxi driver was immediately familiar with the location given by our caller and warned that those meeting us would take precautions to keep their location secret. This turned out to be an accurate assessment of what we were getting into because as soon as we got to our location, we were met by an unmarked van. As soon as we got out of the cab, we were blindfolded, and our phones were taken away.

Our new driver assured us that what was happening was standard procedure to protect the location of the caller's residence. Needless to say, allowing ourselves to be blindfolded by a stranger in Gaza felt very weird. I remembered our conversation with Amit about the incident in Akko, where a tourist was in the wrong place at the wrong time. Now, here we were going to who-knows-where—blindfolded. There was something uniquely unnerving about being swept away in an unmarked vehicle, knowing that no one had a clue where we were going to be. It was hard not to think of the worst-case scenario.

Our arrival some twenty minutes later caused a stir. We could hear whispering as we were led out of the van, and it wasn't until we had been led for quite some way that the blindfolds were finally removed. We found ourselves inside a small warehouse. We'd been taken inside a tiny room where

The Companion

antiquities lined the walls. Were we at a collector's home? Or maybe everything we were looking at was stolen property?

Several men were trying to light a stove with a natural gas canister to take the chill out of the morning air. The man's lighter didn't work, however, and I was further disturbed by the smell of gas leaking into the room. I wondered if we were going to be one of those unexplained explosions in Gaza on the evening news. I look at Pieta and his expression told me he was thinking something similar. Our hosts had positioned us into a corner of the room beside a closet. We squeezed our bodies into the corner and wonder what we'd gotten ourselves into. Finally, the flame ignited after the man lit a match and Pieta and I breathed a sigh of relief. The men were speaking Hebrew, ignoring us completely.

The door on the far side of the warehouse opened and a dark silhouette of a bearded man appeared. The closer he got to us the more we could make out his features. He was a burly, dark-skinned man whose full beard hid his mouth as he spoke.

"Welcome to my humble collection," he said. "My name is Hadi Zahir and I am the owner of all that you see here. It is my understanding that you seek information about the discovery of a piece of Mamluke pottery that resurfaced in 2007."

Pieta spoke up without hesitation. "Yes," he said. "We've heard it was discovered at a gravesite just outside of Akko."

"That is true," Hadi said. "If I remember correctly, your piece was from the twelfth century," he said.

"We are still a little confused about the pottery's journey since its discovery in 1971," I said.

"You foreigners come here and think we will turn over our secrets just like that," he said gruffly. It was difficult to tell what Hadi thought about our being in Gaza and our reasons for being there. His facial expression was hard to read with the beard, so we were left to interpret whatever we could from the inflection in his voice. I immediately felt nervous, and again went back to my worst case scenario. We had no idea who this man was, and here we were prying him for information.

"If I am to answer your questions, you will be expected to answer mine about the dream text," he said.

"Of course," Pieta said. "We will tell you everything we've learned since we arrived in Israel." "I can tell you," Hadi said, "that the piece was in a local museum until it was stolen in 1983. After that it went underground and stayed a mystery until recently."

The more Hadi spoke the more our fear subsided. He explained the tale of the Mamluke pottery, filling in some blanks left out of Natalie's description of events.

"The pottery itself, of course, isn't nearly as significant as what was found inside it," Hadi said. "It seems it was a profound spiritual text, yes? And yet it would have never been found if the pottery hadn't been broken in transit."

"Transit?" Pieta asked.

"Yes, the wife of the thief who stole the pottery finally decided to try to sell the piece in 2007, and she decided to bring the pottery to an art dealer. The piece broke at some point along the way, and when she found the text, she thought maybe the art dealer would still be interested in purchasing it. It turns out the art dealer did not overlook the text's importance, and this is how it resurfaced and why you know what you know about its existence."

Pieta and I had been nervous upon arrival, but the more Hadi talked the more engaged in the journey of the text I became.

The Companion

"Local interpreters say that the text is the Book of Job, described as a dream. I have spoken to a friend of mine who has a connection to the art dealer. He got a glimpse of the text before it was sold to someone in the United States. I can tell you what he shared with me."

Hadi explained how he became enlightened through his own self-discovery. He had been studying the ancient Kabbalah for years and was particularly interested in the wisdom teachings of the text. He explained that his name, "Hadi Zahir," means "bright guiding light" in Arabic.

Pieta and I glanced at each other and a knowing look of relief passed between us. We had no reason to be afraid. Our host was one of us.

"What did your friend say about the manuscript?" Pieta asked.

"He told me that the author of the dream might have been a twelfth-century Kabbalist," Hadi answered. "I am Arabic, but study the Kabbalah. It's my belief that the Kabbalah helps explain the collision between Jews and Arabs. I asked my friend what the document had to say about the shadow aspect of the ego as a companion."

"Companion?" Pieta asked, a puzzled expression crossing his face. "We weren't aware that the text covered the shadow."

Hadi nodded. "My friend told me that the document describes how the ego destroys the human spirit by working on our insecurities. Ego does this until our very ground is washed away. Though we hold out emotionally for a short time, eventually we lose confidence in our heart's convictions."

We were both impressed at Hadi's ability to articulate in English his friend's interpretation. We later discovered that he was educated in the United States.

The Astonishing Dream of JOB

"That is my sense as well," Pieta said. "It's as though we are being warned not to fear the ego because it just makes it stronger."

"It also makes our self-talk all-consuming," I said.

"It makes you wonder," Hadi said. "What did Job know at the time that the rest of the world didn't? What did he feel was happening to him?"

"The better question," Pieta responded, "is why did Job elevate his heart's truth above his fear? And, how did he know that we have a greater purpose as human beings than a life that is submissive to ego?"

"Well, we know from the ego's perspective that we can never be perfect," I said. "My sense of this 3,600-year-old message is that we are fated to be consumed by our own disapproval."

"I think Job was telling us that true wisdom does not hide its source," Hadi said. "Everyone who lives life somehow knows this. In other words, experience is our best teacher."

There were moments during this conversation that I lost track of where in the world we were: the Middle East. That changed, however, as soon as Hadi spoke about the lost confidence of his people.

"When our thoughts are full of dread," he said, "and peace is present, we imagine that something will enter and ruin it. We do not believe that we can come out of the dark into light, but instead defend ourselves around every corner. When we repeatedly have this as our life experience, it is hard not to believe that darkness is close by."

We were moved by Hadi's passion. It was clear that this document was not only important to those of us from the West. Everyone seemed to be hoping for a deeper understanding of how we could be better human beings—especially to one another.

"Yes," Pieta added. "Many of us live in fear and are so consumed by stress that we quickly ready ourselves in self-defense. The text suggests that in this moment we are actually preparing to defend our ego—not our heart's truth."

"What is so moving about the discovery of this text is that we no longer have to vainly believe there is nothing that can be done to save ourselves. This would be a mistake," Hadi said.

"A mistake?" I asked.

"My understanding is," he answered, "that the ego wants us to ignore our heart's truth. Doing so causes us to create a dark version of ourselves. Imagine a life sentence in which every human being is ashamed for simply existing. Job's experience of despair teaches us that this would be a horrible mistake. We actually have another option."

"Yes," Pieta replied. "We can choose to trust our heart's intelligence."

"We start out having the personal resources to be all we can in life," I added. "But, the ego breaks our spirit. Attacking our thoughts and manipulating our emotions, it wounds us where we are the most vulnerable. The experience literally empties our worth onto the ground."

"Yes, suffering with ego distortions can cause human beings to insulate themselves for protection," Pieta said. "The human spirit becomes swollen with grief and many of us don't even know why we are grieving. Simply put, it's the loss of self."

"This is why I am interested in the dream text," Hadi said. "I understand the interpretation teaches that our suffering does not have to be in vain. It can, in fact,

The Astonishing Dream of JOB

transform us if we view the ego as a companion rather than the enemy."

"That is profound," I said. "The heart is connected to consciousness and truth. Developing a reciprocal relationship with the ego means the heart could be our compass when we awaken. Imagine that!"

"Yes," Pieta said excitedly. "Our perceptions of the truth are dim because of ego embarrassment. It drains our physical energy. Everyone has the same battle in spiritual work. There is no need for pride to get in the way. If I can add to what Hadi is saying, we do not have to remain passive in our relationship with the ego. If we do, that passivity becomes our personal hell. And, this is a source of depression for a lot of people."

I thought about this for a moment. Passivity's greatest damage is done within the mind of the individual who is ruled by it. Thus, what starts as a self-protective mechanism to avoid injury, or perhaps just an easy out from responsibility, turns into a bondage that ultimately destroys the human personality. It can cripple an individual's ability to love or to care about anything.

"It is my feeling that to love at all is to be vulnerable," I said. "What you're describing happens because many people push their feelings into the unconscious to quiet their angst to be. Sadly, repression evolves into depression."

"So, then, do you agree that making the ego our companion is better than rejecting or denying its existence?" Hadi asked.

"Absolutely," Pieta answered. "It becomes shadow because it was rejected in the first place. Darkness is a form of self-defense. Eventually befriending this quality allows us to convert or to transform it. Then it serves us rather than the other way around."

The Companion

"What are your thoughts about the text implying that Job was possessed by an inner genie?" Hadi asked.

"Genies?" I thought to myself. "What the—?" I glanced at Pieta, who didn't seem surprised by Hadi's question.

"Most are not aware," Hadi said, "but these supernatural creatures were believed to occupy a parallel world to ours. Together with humans and angels they make up one of the three sentient creations of God or Allah."

"You are the first person I've come across on my journey to mention genies," Pieta answered. "I have a friend, someone who has seen the text as well, who suggested to me that Job was warned that his perceptions and free will were trapping him on a path that opposes ego. He also felt that a genie was the source of his opposition. What a coincidence."

"The belief in genies is part of Arabic culture," Hadi said. "Maybe your friend is Arabic, or has studied our culture."

"Wow!" I said. "I never knew that angels and genies were considered as equals in the Arabic culture."

"Yes," Pieta replied. "According to the Qur'an there are two creations that have free will: humans and genies. The Qur'an mentions that genies were made of a smokeless flame, and that they formed communities, just like humans, and, like humans, they can be good or bad."

"It's interesting," Hadi continued. "Scholars feel someone is abandoning their religion when they disbelieve in one of God's creations; meanwhile, it's largely acceptable to believe in angels, but not so much so to believe in genies."

"Fascinating," Pieta remarked. "It's been my feeling all along that Job was being guided by something other than his heart. I had concluded it was a divine source—the Soul. It seems we can add a genie to the list of possibilities as well."

The Astonishing Dream of JOB

"Uh, I guess so," I said in disbelief. "That's certainly a new concept for me."

As the conversation shifted from the text, I couldn't help but wonder about the antiquities all around us. "Uh," I said sheepishly, finally asking the question I'd been wanting to ask since arriving. "Are these antiquities all yours?"

"Yes they are," Hadi said with pride. "I own a construction company and we keep whatever we dig up. Rather than turn the treasures over to the museums, I collect them and sell them to third parties." He told us that Gaza does not have laws regarding rescued archaeology. When construction crews happened on archaeological artifacts, they got to keep what they find.

I couldn't have been happier that my first impressions of Hadi were wrong. Feeling more comfortable, I asked him about the security measures in bringing us here.

"The general public is not aware of art crime and its impact on society at large," Hadi said. "It's a multi-billion dollar legitimate industry, with a conservatively estimated $6 billion annual profit. I have to protect myself, and go to extreme measures if and when I choose to bring new people here. Since the Second World War, art crime has evolved from a relatively innocuous crime, into the third highest-grossing annual criminal trade worldwide."

"Well, that explains things," I said. It was getting late, and I wondered if our visit would end soon. I wondered how we were going to get back to town. Would we be blindfolded again? Had our host become comfortable enough to trust us in knowing his whereabouts?

"Will spiritual seekers in the West accept the idea that Job's experience was a dream?" Hadi asked.

"Dreams with a religious or spiritual nature go back as far as the written word," Pieta replied. Some of the earliest records on dream interpretation were written in cuneiform on clay tablets as early as the 7th century B.C. I don't think people in our section of the world will have trouble accepting this document."

Pieta leans in closer to Hadi. "Can you show me the rest of your collection? I am looking for a very specific artifact. I've been told it is unique to this area of the world."

"Of course, of course," Hadi nodded. "I would be glad to show you my collection."

"Artifact?" I thought. This must be what Pieta was seeking. He'd told me everything would soon make sense. I was excited and curious to find out what it was, but knowing Pieta, I knew better than to dig for more information.

Instead, I turned my attention back to Hadi and the conversation about dreams. "In ancient times, dreams, especially the dreams of rulers," I said, "often were considered a direct communication with God. Westerners are very curious about their dreams. Certainly, the depth of Job's experience is much more profound when seen from this perspective. Wouldn't you agree?"

"Yes. I remember my mother reading us the dream story of Jacob's ladder," Hadi said. "It supposedly reached from the earth to heaven, with angels climbing and descending it. I loved that image as a child."

"When did we stop listening to dreams?" I asked.

"Sadly, dreams fell into disfavor with the Christian church just before the Dark Ages," Pieta answered. "There are some who think that their disapproval had to do with so many ancient texts being mistranslated, and so they deemed the dreams within them as witchcraft."

"My attraction to dreams is rooted in Jungian psychology," I said. "Jung felt that the symbolism or archetypes were patterns from within the collective

The Astonishing Dream of JOB

unconscious that guide our psyche toward a state of wholeness."

"Yes," Pieta nodded. "If I remember correctly, he related human transformation to a symbolic death and rebirth, a death of the existing ego state in order for the new self to emerge or be born. I get the feeling that this is what happened to Job."

"What do you mean by that?" Hadi asked.

"Job's suffering begins when he tries to abandon a view of himself that doesn't match his heart's perspective," Pieta explained. "He is essentially trapped by an impending storm of emotions that takes him into a place of despair. This is a symbolic death that is followed by a period of searching for a new self."

"Ahhh," Hadi said. "So he is turning inward to confront his negative self?"

"Exactly!" Pieta said. "He is encountering the conflict between his opposing sides — heart versus ego. This is the natural balancing force within the psyche that is attempting to reintegrate a fragmented self."

Hadi nodded.

"Unfortunately," Pieta explained, "religious leaders in the States do not acknowledge our ability to receive messages from God or a divine source. Even science doesn't support the value of dreams, considering them to be junk we need to sort out from our day."

"The truth is, they often point the way to our spiritual growth," Hadi replied.

Our conversation had lasted much longer than I originally thought. It was becoming clear that Pieta's agenda was to get Hadi to give us a tour of his collection. As the evening closed, we discussed accounts of psychic events in the Bible. Pieta reminded us that Joseph's insightful interpretations of the Pharaoh's dreams helped him avert the consequences of a disastrous plague.

We asked Hadi if we could meet the friend he'd told us about.

"I would be honored to connect you with my friend," he answered. "His name is Rabbi Karim Marish. He is an inspiring advocate of this dream's messages. I will instruct my driver to take you there tomorrow morning. Meanwhile, will you be my guest this evening?"

The offer was refreshing since I was exhausted and had no desire to get back into the van and be transported across town blindfolded. "We are flattered," Pieta said. "And can we still look at your collection?"

"Yes, of course," Hadi said. "It is rare that my home and collection is open to viewers."

We spent the next hour asking Hadi about his work and how he had become a collector. Afterwards, Pieta and I knew that if tomorrow was anything like today, we were going to need to get some rest.

The Astonishing Dream of JOB

The Companion

6

Spiritual Truths

51. Unconscious ego (shadow), consisting of repressed weaknesses, shortcomings, and instincts, are to be viewed as a companion.

52. Fearing ego only makes it stronger.

53. True wisdom comes from "suffering with" our life experiences.

54. Consumed in fear, we live in a state of self-defense.

55. Ignoring our heart's truth creates a darker version of the self—shadow.

56. The human spirit swells with grief about our lost self.

57. A reciprocal relationship with ego means we've restored the heart as our compass.

58. Passivity or accepting an egoic fate can become our personal hell.

59. Befriending the shadow converts or transforms it to serve us.

60. Heart versus ego is a natural balancing principle within the psyche.

The Astonishing Dream of JOB

7

Humbled by the Ego

Hadi had told us that the only visitors to Gaza were intrepid journalists and humanitarian organizations that risked their safety to come here. We were a different breed, he'd said, seekers who wanted a deeper spiritual understanding of an ancient text. Somehow this didn't make me feel any safer. Our quest was now sending us back north and to a section of Israel where the ethnic makeup was 99.2% Jewish and non-Arab. I, for one, felt relieved by this since Gaza had a history of Arab conflict and bombings.

We were to meet Hadi's friend, a rabbi, in the small town of Safed, 118 miles from Gaza. In the Northern District of Israel, Safed is considered to be one of Judaism's four holy cities and has remained a center of Kabbalah.

Hadi escorted us into town, asking permission to maintain the privacy of his location by blindfolding us. "Just as much for your protection as mine," he said. "There are many unscrupulous people in this city who would love to know the whereabouts of my collection." Fully understanding Hadi's worries, we agreed. We remained blindfolded for the full thirty minutes until we reached Gaza.

The Astonishing Dream of JOB

The city of Gaza is sheltered by sand dunes from the sea, which are not visible from the town. We were on a road that led down to the shore, where there was a landing pier. Pieta decided en route that traveling by land to Safed was going to be fraught with security checks and possible detainment, so he opted to hire a boat. Unfortunately, hiring a boat was not as easy as it might have seemed. Every time Pieta was on the verge of reaching an agreement with a boat owner, the contract fell through. Hadi told us that this was likely due to outside political pressures. After all, we were Americans wanting an escort into international waters. Though it was very difficult to arrange, we finally pushed forward and secured a boat and captain.

By the time we left Gaza it was 6:30 p.m. Much of our day had been spent eating breakfast at Hadi's home, talking about his collection, and then preparing for our blindfolded trek into Gaza. Finally, here we were, and now we were dickering over the boat. Before departing the docks, we bid Hadi farewell and promised we would relay any new information discovered from his friend the rabbi. As our boat left the pier and headed north along the coast, we reflected about our brief visit to Gaza and our time with Hadi.

"Certainly, no one aware of Israel's blockade of goods and services to Gaza, or Israel's devastating bombing of Gaza, would consider this a vacation haven," Pieta said.

"No," I said. "It's not a place of joy."

Pieta continued, "I saw in the paper that journalists consider it an overcrowded war zone populated by more than a million terrified men, women, and children."

"Yes," I replied. "It is hard to imagine that they subsist here amidst the rubble. Here you have a tiny strip of land that can be driven across in two hours, and no space for recreation. No scenic boulevards or tiny cafes. Even their beach is dangerous."

"It's very sad," Pieta said. "These peoples' lives are a daily challenge, filled with fear and emotional wounds."

As we entered international waters, we were told by our captain that Israel controls the waters off Gaza's coast and that they routinely blocked ships from coming into the Palestinian territory. We were glad to be going in the opposite direction.

***

The Mediterranean coastline of Israel is beautiful as it extends 118 miles from Gaza to Rosh Hanikra. It is a combination of sandy beaches, sandstone, mountain ranges, and rocky cliffs. The cliffs of Akko were the visual cue that we were close to our destination. Pieta was correct. The boat trip did turn out to be much faster than the road. Coming into the Port of Haifa, we were only a short drive from the town of Safed. Securing a car shortly after arriving, we had to drive thirty-two hundred feet above sea level and into the mountains of Upper Galilee, where the views were incredible.

"Can you believe that for the longest time Safed was a well-kept secret, even to most Israelis?" Pieta asked.

"How so?" I asked.

"According to the great mystics of the past, Safed will play an important role in the final redemption scenario. It is said that the Messiah will come from Safed on his way to Jerusalem. It has something to do with a third temple needing to be built here. Some even believe that God's presence rests above Safed."

Pieta explained that Safed was founded in 70 AD. The city flourished in the sixteenth century, a time when many famous Jewish religious scholars and mystics moved there fleeing from the horrors of the Inquisition. Safed ultimately became the spiritual center of the Jewish world, where Kabbalah, Jewish mysticism, reached their peak of influence. "It sounds like we are in the right place to continue our journey," I said. "Here we are meeting a rabbi and it is rumored that the author of our dream interpretation may actually be a twelfth-century Kabbalist!"

"Yes," Pieta answered. "Safed is famous for its great teachers and mystics. I'm humbled by the possibilities of what we may discover next."

Safed is one of four holy cities in Israel, together with Jerusalem, Hebron, and Tiberias. The oldest part of town consists of narrow cobblestone alleys with artists' galleries, medieval synagogues, private homes, and small guest houses.

"You can feel the Jewish soul here," Pieta said. "Someone could come here and totally immerse themselves in Torah study."

"This mountain air is unbelievable," I mused. "It certainly is a place for clear thinking and meditation. I've never been anywhere that offers such seclusion and serenity, the very conditions needed for powerful spiritual experiences."

"Yes," Pieta replied. "Safed is where the spiritual meets the physical and Eastern thought and Western thought come together. I have a sense that today is going to be quite an experience."

Once we got our bearings, Pieta pulled out the notes he had taken with Hadi's very specific instructions: "Park your car at Jerusalem Street by Rothschild Garden. Walk straight until you pass the garden at Safed College. There you will come to a paved street on your right. Walk to the top and you will be at the Jewish Quarter. Look for two houses with the numbers 47 and 49. They will be on your right. Between them will be a narrow staircase known as Messiah Alley.

Humbled by the Ego

Take this staircase until you come to Simta Beit Street then turn left onto Hassidim. This last right will lead you to Ma'alot Gure Ha'Ari. You are now above the Ashkenazic Synagogue. The rabbi will meet you at the bottom of the stairs."

We followed the instructions carefully until we spotted Rabbi Karim Marish, who was waiting for us in the designated spot. At a single glance it was obvious how strongly he'd been shaped and influenced by the past: the history of his family and the Jewish people as a whole was written all over his weathered face.

"Good morning! Good morning!" called Rabbi Marish. "I worried whether Hadi's directions would get you here. I am glad to meet you!"

"We would not have missed this opportunity for the world," Pieta said.

"Hadi tells me we have a common interest?" he said, inflecting his voice with a question even though I was sure he and Hadi had discussed the texts.

"Yes," Pieta replied. "Hadi told us that you have seen the document that we seek. Is this true?"

Rabbi Marish nodded, but was in no hurry to broach the subject matter we were here to discuss. Instead he began speaking about his education in the United States. Clearly we were going to have to calm our excitement, as Rabbi Marish was on his own schedule.

"I attended public school in Milwaukee and went to yeshiva in Chicago," he told us. "I received my ordination in a small rabbinical seminary there. Now it's one of the largest yeshiva in North America."

"That is wonderful," I said. "I read in one of the travel brochures that Mir Yeshiva in Jerusalem is the largest yeshiva in the world. Did you study there as well?" After some more talk about where the rabbi studied, Pieta was able to gracefully turn the conversation toward the text. As soon as Rabbi Marish got started, we realized this was a man who was as fascinated by the Job dream interpretation as we were.

"You know the shape of the community here in Safed is changing rapidly," he said. "We are an older generation, many of us immigrants, and in passing very few of our children are remaining traditional in their religious practice."

"What does that mean for the future of your community?" I asked.

"Well, there is a small yet strong tide of young adults finding out about and choosing our Orthodox life," he answered. "This is having a profound effect on the community. We are always seeking new ways to connect with non-Orthodox people. And this dream text may assist us greatly."

"How so?" Pieta asked.

"Young people are interested in suffering," he answered. "Mostly how they can avoid it. The dream interpretation guides them in a way that is modern, that they can relate to."

"I don't know what it is like here," Pieta said, "but in the States confusion and shame is at an all-time high. There is a strong need to understand the human dilemma."

"We know from this dream text," the rabbi replied, "that no matter how long it takes to become conscious or how upsetting, the judgment of ego is unsubstantiated."

"I'm glad to hear we agree on that," I said. "Ultimately, the ego cuts us off from our path and blocks our freedom. This cutting is a source of darkness for many people and can foster a life that seems meaningless."

"My understanding," Pieta added, "is that we are inherently ethical in the beginning and aligned with our true nature. But rather than being left to develop naturally, we are provoked by the human spirit."

"Yes," Rabbi Marish answered. "It is this provocation to suffer that many feel is an injustice to mankind. This ancient dream teaches us that the human spirit knows that personal transformation is contingent on our suffering ….it's not being a particular or righteous way that leads to transformation. Essentially, suffering melts the ego's moral character so we can know the ethic of our hearts."

"Is this what ancient alchemists considered when turning lead into gold?" I asked. "Out of the shadow comes our divinity?"

"Yes," said the rabbi. "Sadly, the ego's moral judgments make our emotions seem like the enemy. We actually begin to fear our own feelings. It is no wonder that so many people feel alone and alienated. By learning early on to serve the ego, we fear intimacy, mostly because the ego distorts it. Our natural inner compass becomes inefficient, which leaves our heart defenseless to all sorts of attacks."

"What does the dream interpretation say is the solution?" Pieta asked.

"It is my understanding that Job's heart breaking is the impetus for him wanting his inner experience recorded as a proclamation of how to suffer," the rabbi said. "This makes the dream a profound message to us."

Then Rabbi Marish revealed to us that he had seen a portion of the dream text. This was also how he'd happened to meet the art dealer.

"When the text surfaced a few years ago," he said, "Hadi knew the art dealer who was appraising its worth and wanted to understand its content. He was unable to read much of the Arabic, so Hadi referred him to me. I must admit, at the time, I was unaware that the authorities suspected that the

The Astonishing Dream of JOB

artifacts were stolen property. I was too excited about the find."

"We can certainly understand that!" I said.

"We sure can," Pieta concurred. "So, having seen what you saw, what do you think is the dream's profound message?"

"Simply put," the rabbi answered, "we are to honor our heart's intelligence over the ego."

"That's the problem, isn't it?" asked Pieta. "That's easier said than done. We are so conditioned to respect fear over love, we don't trust our heart."

Rabbi Marish explained that the Ashkenazic Synagogue is one of the most well-known and highly visited places in Safed. "It is a perfect setting for learning the origins of the Kabalistic idea of repairing the world," he said. "Job's message is that egos break the world while hearts repair it."

"My sense is that Job felt in his heart that a higher purpose and intelligence would be revealed to him. Is that accurate?" Pieta asked.

"Yes," he answered. "The Kabbalah teaches that the human soul consists of three parts: physical desire and instinct; the ability to distinguish between good and evil; and specific to humans, our intellect and awareness of the divine. The latter two can be attained only through intentions and actions. When these two components come into full flower, the person has experienced spiritual enlightenment. Clearly, Job is having this experience."

"Can you explain?" I asked.

"Job recognizes that we have an intuitive knowing of a divine connection to creation and the Universe," he answered. "He also believed that in death we shed this body, but our soul lives on in its original form."

Humbled by the Ego

"So this ancient dream is profound because it suggests our soul orchestrates and guides our lives?" Pieta asked. "And it does this whether we are conscious of it or not?"

"Yes!" the Rabbi answered. "And it also does so without judgment. Job feels that we, not the ego, determine the ethical implications of our existence. He is arguing that our heart is the compass!"

"THAT is profound!" Pieta said. "This means when our emotional self undergoes a rebirth there is a reconnection with our heart. The next evolution is to connect to the higher self or the divine."

"Yes!" the Rabbi said again. "This text recognizes that our higher self is connected to the heart. This is Job's message in a moment of despair. It is here that he learns that our longing is not just for love but for peace from ego judgments."

"How sad is it that so much harm and neglect impairs our emotional development?" Pieta said. "Our feelings are such an important piece of who we are."

"It seems the ego's judgment was intended to control people who may become misguided," he answered, explaining the ego's role in the human condition. "Particularly those people who live their lives at the expense of others. The ego creates the illusion that moral judgment is always present."

"So, intuitively the soul desires that we be embodied and sense the importance of our emotional development, but it realizes that we will be exposed to the ego's guilt no matter what?" I asked.

"Yes," the Rabbi answered. "If not learned from your parents, you will get it from the culture."

"This guilt so confuses people," Pieta said angrily. "It's as though we are to follow a specific set of rules to become whole when in truth it is a process of understanding who and what we are. If we get stuck in the mistakes of our youth, guilt and shame becomes the source of our dis-ease."

"The human spirit is actually the antagonist that provokes the ego's dis-ease into awareness," I said, remembering the rabbi's earlier comments about personal transformation and suffering.

"Yes," said the rabbi. "This is a profound point of the text. If not for the human spirit forcing Job awake, he would have been poisoned with dis-ease or fear forever. He would never have known the richness of his own life."

"Because we are examining Job's experience as an internal reaction to an outside event, we are witnessing various stages of his spiritual growth," I said excitedly. "This is much more useful than a theology question of why bad things happen to good people."

"Especially since we've yet to hear from anyone who has seen this ancient dream in its entirety," Pieta added.

"There is much we do know from the dream text," the rabbi said. "We must examine our own suffering. Though it's unconscious, if kept out of awareness, our suffering will be experienced as the dis-ease of fear."

"And, at some level," Pieta added, "it is predetermined that those of us spirited enough to go against this abuse of power by the ego will be viewed as black sheep by the culture and harshly judged by it."

Rabbi Marish told us that throughout history spiritual or religious discoveries, such as this dream text, were revealed only to a chosen few. No one in ancient times was considered pious enough to learn such hallowed secrets. Now, however, society's shift in consciousness, largely due to technology, allows such information to be heard by anyone who is seeking it.

"History teaches us, however," the rabbi said, "that when spiritual enlightenment is revealed, not everyone necessarily flocks to the path."

"Yeah. Why is that?" I asked.

"Religious texts say that true spiritual understanding is rare," he answered. "One of the most widely respected spiritual books in India, The Bhagvat Gita, states that of thousands of men, only a few undertake the spiritual road, and of those, only a few gain understanding."

"Yes, and doesn't the Bible claim that reaching heaven is as difficult as a camel passing through the eye of a needle?" Pieta mused.

"So, I guess it's entirely reasonable for an ordinary human to question the usefulness of becoming enlightened," I said. "In the end, do you think the potency of Job's message will be able to reach the masses?"

"I do!" he answered emphatically. "A powerful remedy is needed to heal the world of estrangement and alienation. I believe this new and contemporary discussion of Job's story as an inner experience is a valuable perspective on human suffering. If the sanctity of the Book of Job is reduced from its biblical status as a result of this interpretation, what does it matter if it heals and inspires people today?"

"Do you not think that some of the problem comes from the fact that many people do live their lives at the expense of others?" I asked. "And, they seem to do so without consequence? In fact, some people are famous for living like that."

"Yes," the Rabbi answered. "Egos without fear or guilt get planted in the consciousness of man more often than advocates of love and compassion. Selfishness skews the perception of every generation. Power and fear rule, while love is passive. This illusion of power is allowed to manifest in the culture, and we call its proponents gurus."

"Yes, but such people are missing a genuine experience in their hearts. Egos can just as quickly lose everything," Pieta added. "The problem with ego worship is that it will abandon us with no sense of how or why it happened. Love does not."

"Spiritual teacher and author Eckhart Tolle writes that the ego's inability to recognize itself and see what it's doing is staggering and unbelievable," I said. "And, to become free of it, all we need to do is to be aware of our thoughts and emotions—as they happen."

"Yes," Pieta adds. "So, here we have a contemporary spiritual teacher offering a strategy to free ourselves from the ego's influence that entered consciousness 3,600 years ago. Amazing."

"Exactly!" I answered. "By making the shift from thinking to awareness, Job discovered intelligence far greater than the ego. Our challenge today is to practice this strategy in our daily lives. We've certainly wasted enough time observing the ego judging itself."

Pieta smiled. "In truth," he said, "for all the time we worry about and feed the ego, no one gets out of this experience alive—especially the ego!"

***

It was a beautiful day outside and Rabbi Marish informed us that he needed to go to the marketplace to stock the kitchen in the synagogue. We decided this would be a good excuse to take a break, or at least to continue our discussion while walking. I was excited to meet some of the locals.

We had heard complaints about panhandlers from other Americans who had come to Safed. We were told they would be aggressive, insistent, and abrasive, but this was not our

Humbled by the Ego

experience. Rabbi Marish told us that the percentage of people begging for handouts was modest.

"The idea that they are aggressive," he said, "couldn't be further from the truth. You will see."

Our walk along the cobblestone streets brought us to Sarah, a woman sitting outside the town bakery. She told us she'd once been an English teacher in her native Russia. She immigrated to Israel more than a dozen years ago. Rabbi Marish stepped inside to buy some bread.

"I can barely make it on my small pension," Sarah told us. "I stretch it the best I can to cover my basic expenses." Rabbi Marish reached into his pockets for some coins as he exited the bakery.

"It seems to me that Job is questioning whether we can place the heart's intelligence above the ego," Pieta said, shifting the conversation back to his main area of interest. "Or he's asking if we are to have a reciprocal relationship with the ego, what is it supposed to look like?"

"Yeah, and to make matters worse, if fear forms our self-perception, then we're trapped," I added. "What a predicament."

"In truth, anxiety is the ego's secret," the rabbi answered, eyeing the marketplace for where to go next. "And it does not consider our three-dimensional existence."

"Wait!" Pieta said. "You're right. The ego is stuck between the poles of right and wrong. It can only see our life two-dimensionally."

"Yes!" answered the rabbi. "Here we can understand Job's resistance. The ego has no middle ground. It does not know compromise or compassion."

The Astonishing Dream of JOB

"So then," Pieta continued, "if we awaken to the illusions of ego, we can find peace and realize our potential. Meanwhile, suffering is a given in the human condition."

"But, if seen from the heart's perspective," I said, "we can suffer with ourselves and be transformed?"

"Yes!" the Rabbi answered. "Another profound message: once we have been humbled by ego, we will then be rescued by ego."

"This is an important distinction," I said. "Humbled by ego means if we suffer with its outdated and false messages, we transform the self. Rescued means mindful of the transformation we can now live in the present."

"That's right," answered the Rabbi. "The mystery Job wanted resolved initially was about where our internal judge resides. We know now it is in our thoughts. He also wondered if we were allowed to examine thought and its effect on our lives. The answer, of course, is yes, because now these are our cultural beliefs."

"Absolutely amazing!" I said. "Everything that was restricted by the collective ego since the beginning of Western thought is allowed today. Why do we not live our lives as if these truths exist?"

"Ah," said the rabbi. "Examine the evidence throughout history. If one looks at the shadow side of religious teachings, they are severely ostracized."

"Yes," Pieta added. "And if we try to validate our divinity, these very thoughts and beliefs get in the way."

***

We approached a man named Yakov as we walked on, another regular on Main Street who Rabbi Marish knew. He had a chair that one of the shops kept for him. The rabbi told us that he was out daily, sitting outside the pharmacy selling little knick-knacks. The small plastic bracelets and necklaces had to be worth pennies, but even so a few people buy them. I wanted to look inside for sunglasses, as I had lost mine in the desert a few days earlier.

"He passes his time by reciting psalms," Rabbi Marish explained. "When someone passes, if he can catch their eye, he will offer them a blessing."

"What's your mother's name?" Yakov asks Pieta.

With this information, Yakov blesses him and asks for a few shekels in return.

"Most people like the idea of an extra blessing," the rabbi said, smiling. "After all, a blessing never hurts."

I went inside to purchase sunglasses, and when I came outside Pieta and the rabbi were back on the topic of the ego.

"Consciousness provides us with the ego's intent," Pieta was saying. "And, if suffered with correctly, awakening will activate our hearts. We're so overwhelmed with fear that we don't trust this as an option."

Pieta and Rabbi Marish were leaning on a wall in the shade as I approached them. I wished I had remembered to bring my camera. It would have made a wonderful picture. As I approached, Rabbi Marish turns toward me.

"Did you find your glasses?" he asked.

"Yes, thank you." I replied.

With that he turned back to Pieta and answered his question by nodding. "That is how the ego tries to keep order within the unconscious. It affects our moods and removes us from our greatest dreams. Everyone's reality is vulnerable to its influence. If we are asleep to this quality in ourselves, it will encompass every thought and reduce our faith to nothing."

The Astonishing Dream of JOB

"Does this suffering not cause our spiritual rebirth?" I asked. "Is this what you mean by softening the heart?"

"Yes, suffering has an accumulative effect on our lives," he answered. "And its wisdom is spread throughout the psyche. But, as the soul is healed of these initial wounds, we become present enough to rebirth our lives."

"I think the most powerful message we can glean from the text is that the human heart will not deceive us if we are paying attention!" Pieta said.

We had circled back to the synagogue by this point and found a man sitting in the front foyer. The rabbi told us that the man's name was Aryie and that he came to sit at the steps every day.

"He collects money for a local charity," the rabbi said. "Meanwhile, he teaches the tourists about the Torah."

"You know what it says about the Sabbath?" Aryie was telling a tourist as we approached. "It says 'Keep the Sabbath Holy.'"

Even after the tourist had given him coins, Aryie continued. "We Jewish people are obligated to keep the Sabbath, to honor it, and to respect its laws. After all, that's why we're all still Jewish today."

Although most people walked past Aryie without stopping, he was able to draw many people to stop and listen.

"The ego has taught us throughout history that there is a portion of the human race that uses fear and judgment as an excuse to become violent," Pieta said. "Some have even suggested that this is our true nature, inherently hostile rather than compassionate. We know now this is our ego's nature."

Humbled by the Ego

"Yes," answered the rabbi. "We learn that the ego spares no one from the process of self-recovery. The more we resist its role in our life, the stronger it becomes."

Rabbi Marish offered to let us read his notes from the dream text at his office the following day. This meant we would finally see verbatim copies of the original text of the dream interpretation. Our excitement was difficult to hide. As the evening came to a close, Rabbi Marish gave us directions to the hostel where we were going to spend the night.

"I will meet you here again tomorrow," he said. "What time should I expect you?"

"Could we meet at 9 a.m.?" Pieta asked.

Rabbi Marish opened the door to the synagogue. "Nine in the morning it is," he said. "I will be here early. Knock on the door loudly as my office is in the back."

We both imagined that neither of us would sleep well knowing what was coming. Little did we know that tomorrow would bring us the missing piece Pieta had been seeking.

The Astonishing Dream of JOB

7
Spiritual Truths

61. The ego cuts us off from our path and blocks our freedom.
62. We are inherently moral but must learn an ethic for our nature.
63. We are provoked by the human spirit to suffer a transformation, not achieve perfection.
64. Message in an emotional storm: honor our heart's intelligence over the ego.
65. The human heart is the compass for an ethical life.
66. Our longing is not for love but for peace from ego judgments.
67. Ego judgments were intended to control those who live their lives at the expense of others.
68. The human spirit is the antagonist, provoking the ego to cause human dis-ease, then transformation.
69. Once we have been humbled by unconscious ego (asleep) we will be rescued by consciousness itself (awakened).
70. Consciousness provides us with the ego's intent and if suffered with correctly it will activate our divinity.

The Astonishing Dream of JOB

8

The Human Spark

We had spent very little time exploring the shops and restaurants in Safed, and I was anxious to explore some old bookstores. So in the morning we ventured to the market area for breakfast and a bit of sightseeing before we met with the rabbi. As soon as we arrived at the synagogue, Pieta wasted no time getting back to our previous conversation.

"By now I'm sure you've guessed that we are somewhat obsessed with this dream text?" Pieta asked.

"Yes, it is clearly consuming your thoughts," the rabbi said, smiling.

"We have one major point to uncover," Pieta said. "Maybe then you will understand the reason for our passion." Rabbi Marish nodded for Pieta to continue.

"We have learned thus far that our divine potential lies in the unconscious and is only accessed if we undergo transformative suffering," Pieta said. "But there is something blocking this discovery in our culture. We have spent our careers assisting others who are undergoing trauma and have learned that there is a specific and healthy way to handle adversity. The hope is that the dream text sheds some light on this."

"In fact, it does," the rabbi answered. "But it speaks of it as a process. For example, we learn that the soul orchestrates what we need to see to gain confidence. This is the beginning."

"The process is developmental then," I said. "This has been our assumption all along, but it seems to elude so many. What does the dream text suggest?"

"It not only tells us to stick with our heart's intelligence, but also to know that the ego's default emotion is fear," he explained. "Once we understand this we no longer have to be afraid."

"Then, once we're unafraid," I asked, "we can make better choices and be in less turmoil?"

"Yes," he answered. "Emotions divide us during our inner journey. We can be overtaken by our suffering. If it's doing what it's supposed to do, suffering can actually melt or dissolve old false versions of the self. This ends the undesirable portion of ego."

"So one would lose old images of his or her identity?" Pieta asked. "Would a person's sense of 'I' and 'me' be changed forever?"

"Absolutely!" the rabbi answered. "Resolving our fear means we can unlock and understand the unconscious. Within this raw material is our divine truth. We know now, because of this dream text, that the human spirit does not know the way. Instead, it's responsible for provoking the ego into action along the way."

"But the implication is," Pieta added, "that not everyone—or few people at least—are able to transform their ego, correct?"

"Yes and no," the rabbi answered. "I believe the dream's message is that the human spirit is more tenacious than the ego. In fact, its determination for presence is the angst of the human condition. I would agree that not everyone is compelled to understand the source of this angst—but consciousness is attainable for everyone. The soul and spirit knows the way and the heart is the compass."

"I think that's where it's confusing for most people." I said. "Psychology implies that all we need to survive our lives is a healthy ego. Few understand that 'survival' just makes life an endurance test and many people are exhausted."

"Yes," He answers. "That is how it becomes a spiritual problem. Remember, the portion of ego that is dissolved represents false images of the self. These self-images are transformed by pain to provoke the ego awake. The ego is not eliminated but rather changed into a healthier version of itself."

"So, it is more valid to say then, that not everyone will pursue the true self because they're too busy surviving the angst of these false self-images?" I asked.

"Yes!" Pieta adds. "Few people know what a healthy ego is because they've been taught its adaptability. This is certainly important, but the dream text takes us to a deeper level of understanding. Normal or healthy is when our inside world is congruent with the outside word, not the other way around. This is the balance that actually heals the spirit and ultimately becomes the epitome of healthiness."

"It is true," the rabbi adds. "Psychology does teach that a healthy ego is one that has the ability to adapt to its reality and interact with the outside world. Particularly, in a way that accommodates one's instincts and moral beliefs. But, this is one of the more important distinctions coming from the dream text. Job is advocating holding onto what his heart knows—rather than what the ego believes. "

"So, Job is seeking a less rigid or moral attitude toward the self?" I asked. "He is more interested in what feels true for the self versus what is right?"

"Exactly!" the rabbi answers. "When our thoughts, behavior, and beliefs are consistent with what we intuitively 'know' about ourselves—this is the healthier ego. In fact, this is an ego awake or present."

"So we are learning that life is more than just adapting," I added. "It's also about 'becoming' who we truly are. So, the statistic 1 in 1000 or the question of who can attain what Job accomplished is not just about dissolving ego. The dream suggests that it is a rare human that is tenacious enough to endure or see past the ego's fear and be spirited enough to pursue the truest version of themselves?"

"Yes," Pieta sighed knowingly. "Without the human spirit, we wouldn't be driven to pursue self-understanding at all."

Rabbi Marish had been adamant the day before when speaking about the Kabbalah that it was important to look to the source when considering the reliability of transmission of highly esoteric doctrine. He suggested that there is rhetoric of reception that assures reliability when sharing such messages. Our rabbi believed that the author of our dream interpretation was a reliable source.

He went on to explain, that "In ancient oral traditions, if a particular idea was transmitted through reliable sources, and the teacher in question was deemed authoritative, then the content of the transmission was considered to be credible and true. In Job's case, he was the learned informant who was questioning human suffering, and was thought to be communicating his inquiry through an internal investigation. Recorded in the Bible, his message came to our well-respected twelfth-century Kabbalist, who decided to approach the entire transmission as a dream."

"So, it is safe to say that our Kabbalist was gleaning deeper spiritual messages than the original biblical Book of Job suggests?" I asked.

"Yes, most certainly," the rabbi answered. "And, we learn from the dream that evidence of our divine connection is in the human spark. I would explain the spirit as a kinetic spark of two arcs. One ignites the physical organ systems with renewable energy and the other ignites our consciousness, or awareness of self. The dream interpretation says specifically that this spark is the kind of energy that defends us when threatened. The spark knows the tiny details of our lives and improvises or finds ways for us to resolve our fears."

"So then, the human spirit IS the spark!" Pieta answered excitedly.

The rabbi smiled at Pieta, content to see both of us so excited about what was being unveiled.

"The value of this message is priceless," Pieta continued. "It means our spirit begins as a feeling or sense. Then paired with an experience, positive or negative, it becomes emotion—energy that then moves our thoughts around. This suggests our ego not only must deal with external challenges but also with challenges from spiritual energies which press from the inside, demanding expression in our individual lives. And Job was certainly feeling this press during his experience."

"That is what science is beginning to say," I said. "Scientists are defining emotion as 'energy in motion.' We generate and entrain ourselves and others in this field. We are essentially human transmitters and antennae."

"What does the text say about finding wisdom and understanding?" Pieta asked. "If human beings struggle to know the meaning of their journey, and it cannot be found through their desires, then where do we look?"

The rabbi began to tell us an old Jewish story about a man who found it difficult to find his clothes in the morning. "The man was so upset that he was afraid to go to bed at night, fearing that he would not remember where he had put his things the next morning," the rabbi said. "One evening he decided to write down the exact location of each article of clothing as he undressed. He was very pleased with himself when he woke up the next morning to his list by his bedside. He reviewed the list, locating each item as he went along; put each thing on until he was fully dressed. "This is great," he said to himself. "But where in the world am I?" Sages have taught for centuries that the wisdom of one's journey is accomplished through self-discovery."

"Ahhhh!" I said, pondering the rabbi's parable. "Being conscious of how/when the spirit provokes the ego into action means that we can know exactly where we are every moment of the day. Looking inward is where we go initially for understanding."

"Yes!" the rabbi said. "But it is important to discern that this means knowing your own ego. The dream suggests that such understanding is not automatically in the depth of our suffering. And though it may be buried in the unconscious, it is not actively with us. Nor do we find understanding because it is our divine entitlement. Knowing oneself is so precious that it cannot be measured against our potential."

"Wow!" I said. "Listen to that. Wisdom and understanding of our ego isn't inside or with us, nor are we entitled to it. And, no matter our inborn talents or life skills, we still may not get it."

"Yes, so it seems," the rabbi said. "Wisdom does not come out of our emotions, nor is it connected to our power. The dream even suggests that our body cannot hold the energy of wisdom. In fact, the message is that wisdom and understanding come from a hidden place."

"By hidden, you mean an unconscious place?" asked Pieta. "We know it is out of our awareness." The rabbi sighed as he shuffled his notes on the table. I can tell he was growing tired, but I also sensed that Pieta's answer was close. Then suddenly, there it was!

"The dream's message is that wisdom comes from suffering with the ego's fears," the rabbi answered. "And, understanding comes from an evolving avoidance of anything that magnifies that fear. This, of course, is only possible if one learns an evolving and humbling form of self-love—compassion. So, to answer your question, wisdom has to be activated! Like insight . . . something exists where there was nothing before."

"Wait," I said, "this is beginning to sound as if we possess the ingredients for such wisdom—but you're saying something has to happen for it to enter our awareness? How does that work?"

"In the beginning, there is a parental ego that watches over us," he said. "Focused purely on survival, the ego influences our thinking and helps us to be afraid or unafraid. Initially, it seems that we are secretly in the ego's favor as it protects us. Because this outer authority presents itself as 'for' us rather than 'against' us, we submit to its influence unknowingly."

"So, this refers to our first experience with the ego as caretaker?" Pieta asked.

"Yes," he replied. "But the next message is that the ego has covert, unexpressed knowledge about itself. Have you come across this in your discussions of the dream text?"

"Only insofar as we have gleaned that covertly the ego uses fear to control us," Pieta answered. "Is that what you mean?"

"Seems that is only half of the equation," the rabbi replied. "The other half is that the ego can only see our lives two-dimensionally."

"Oh my!" I said. "Like looking at the world as if it was a flat screen?"

"Yeah," Pieta added. "And that's a problem since we live in a three-dimensional world."

"Spiritually, the ego lives in a world of duality," Rabbi Marish continued. "It can only walk between the poles of right or wrong, black and white, good or bad, heaven or hell."

"So by contrast," Pieta said, "the human heart sees the whole of something, meaning it automatically views life three-dimensionally."

"Yes, and compassion for the self makes the duality tolerable until our heart sees the larger picture," the rabbi answered.

The rabbi's comment saddened me. Most people in our culture rarely learn, let alone practice, the kind of compassion needed to see their lives in its entirety. Though a meaningful understanding of life is possible for everyone, it is the exception that actually attains such meaning. We were learning during our time with the rabbi that it is a process: the tenacity of the human spirit to get here; layered awareness of the ego's weaknesses; a heartfelt knowing of truth; ending in a culmination of a humbling self-love that then activates our wisdom. The dream text was providing a recipe and implied that, in fact, everyone has the ingredients to grow into a meaningful life.

***

The Human Spark

It was Friday night, and we did not know that the synagogue with its no-frills auditorium would be filling up for an evening service. We exited the rabbi's office to watch a string people arrive—about ten total. A petite mother sat her three small children as she faced the front. With a melodious soprano voice, she began to sing.

The synagogue contained a bimah, or old table, from which the Torah is read. In front were the Torah ark and a cabinet where the Torah Scrolls were kept. The ark was positioned to face toward Jerusalem. We learned that it was reminiscent of the Ark of the Covenant, which contained the tablets of the Ten Commandments. The rabbi explained that this was the holiest spot in the synagogue. The ark was closed with an ornate curtain that hung outside the ark doors.

There was a lamp that the rabbi told us was continuously lit, called the Eternal Light. It was used as a reminder of the western lamp of the menorah of the Temple in Jerusalem. In front was an elaborate chair named for the prophet Elijah that was only used during certain ceremonies. The entire synagogue was full of decorative artwork. We learned that in Rabbinic and Orthodox traditions, three-dimensional sculptures and depictions of the human body are not allowed, as this is considered idolatry. The seats therefore faced the Torah Ark, and when worshippers stood up to pray or to sing, this was the direction they faced.

"What's she singing?" Pieta whispered curiously. "It is beautiful."

"It is the Kabbalah Shabbat service," the rabbi answered. "They are here this evening to mourn through the Kaddish prayer the loss of loved ones. I'm glad you are here for this, actually. It has been well-noted that the Kaddish is the echo of Job in the prayer book: "Though He slays me, yet will I trust in Him.""

The Astonishing Dream of JOB

I was excited about witnessing yet another real-life connection to the dream text. And though I had Jewish friends, I was not aware of this particular prayer. The rabbi explained that the rules of mourning are equal for men and women in the Jewish tradition except for when it comes to the Kaddish.

"So the women can't say Kaddish?" I asked.

"Actually, there are reports of women saying Kaddish dating back four centuries. After the Holocaust, women throughout Europe said Kaddish. Nonetheless, eight centuries after its regular inclusion in Jewish prayer, women saying Kaddish aloud in Orthodox congregations aren't the norm. Nor do most women answer 'amen.'"

We learned that some people feel very naked when they stand up for the Kaddish. The rabbi explained that it's different in an Orthodox synagogue, where people pray every day and usually have groups of people who are in different stages of grief. In this instance, this woman was the only one coming in for Kaddish and thus the only mourner in the congregation to be standing up.

He explained that customs for reciting the Mourners' Kaddish varied markedly among various communities. In Sephardi synagogues, the custom was that all the mourners stand and chant the Kaddish together. In Ashkenazic synagogues, such as this one, the custom was that one mourner is chosen to lead the prayer on behalf of the rest. I could only imagine the added pressure of standing alone while grieving.

"It's my understanding that the Kaddish is quite difficult to say," Pieta said.

"It is," answered the rabbi.

Just then, the woman on the podium began reciting: "Yitgaddal veyitqaddash shmeh rabba . . . "

The rabbi leaned over to translate and whispered her words to us: "May His great name be exalted and sanctified is God's great name . . . "

"Be' alma di vra khir'uteh . . . "

" . . . in the world which He created according to His will!"

Suddenly a stranger – the only other woman in the synagogue – began shouting. "If you want, I can get my father to say Kaddish for you."

The woman in front continued her prayer, but when she finished, it was apparent that she left holding back tears.

"What happened?" I asked.

"Not everyone is comfortable with being chosen to lead Kaddish," the rabbi said. "She is still quite fragile from her loss. She told me earlier in the week she felt ill-prepared to lead the prayer on behalf of others."

Rabbi Marish further explained that his role is to offer reassurance to those who are grieving and to try to encourage those in mourning that the congregation will be supportive. In this instance, it appeared as if the woman had misinterpreted the shouting, and thus she'd left in embarrassment. I couldn't help but feel sorry for her. The rabbi assured us that she would be okay.

"What is the prayer's meaning?" I asked.

"Kaddish in Aramaic means 'holy,'" he explained. "And the central theme of the prayer is the magnification and sanctification of God's name. In the liturgy, different versions of the Kaddish are used functionally as separators between sections of our services."

"So, you have been working with her, helping her prepare for today's Kaddish?" Pieta asked.

The Astonishing Dream of JOB

"Yes," he answered. "And, if the grief is recent, as it is in her case, it can be difficult. The recitation of Kaddish to honor the dead is a relatively late phenomenon," the rabbi continues. "Most are of the belief that it was in the thirteenth century that the mourner's Kaddish became an established part of Jewish ritual."

The rabbi told us that the opportunity to recite the Kaddish has different meaning for different women. Some are comfortable having others recite the Kaddish for them, but many also feel a deep need to honor their loved ones themselves.

"What is the uniqueness of this particular prayer?" I asked.

"Well, the Mourner's Kaddish has several functions," the rabbi answered. "It blends in with the internal spirit of the mourner, imperceptibly healing his or her psychological wounds, and it teaches the mourner vital and profound lessons about life and death, and the conquest of evil."

"This is related to the dream text, isn't it?" Pieta asked, and smiled.

"What?" I asked with surprise. "How is this related?"

"It seems that during a time when we are consumed with indulgence and insecurities," the rabbi answered, "lessons of life should be making us compassionate. Of course, no one can prescribe the length of time it takes to integrate a loss. But it is our challenge as human beings to suffer with the intolerable burden of intense loneliness that comes with such an experience—then evolve. The inner freezing of the ego should begin to thaw. Isolation from the world of people and the retreat inward begins to relax, and normalcy returns. Compassion or self-love makes this possible."

"There is never a time that we feel more helpless if not during the death of a loved one," Pieta added.

The Human Spark

"True, and imagine what Job went through," I said. "He lost everything!"

Rabbi Marish nodded. "The dream text suggests that compassion is the solution. When we help people who are less fortunate, or people who cannot help themselves, we are immersed in a context of living that can be mirrored by others."

"Do you mean that there is more in life than living out of the ego and simply approaching people with our accomplishments?" Pieta asked.

"Yes," the rabbi answered. "Self-love or suffering with our adversity establishes a context of living that ultimately comforts others and offers hope. Job learns this initially when he gets frustrated with his inner voices. Remember, they were portrayed as his friends Eliphaz the Themanite, Baldad the Suhite, and Sophar the Naamathite. The dream suggests each is strictly an internal character and distinctly different in his presentation and intent. One will guide and support, the other argues and condemns, and the third tries to reach a compromise the other two cannot. This inner dialogue represents Job suffering with himself."

"So what happens to those of us who never discover the ethic of compassion?" I asked.

"The young make fun of peers who are sensitive to their feelings or the distress of others," the rabbi said. "Compassion is often portrayed as a sign of weakness by role models, and it's increasingly difficult to teach in an evolving shame-based culture. We're seeing what happens. The young have little guidance."

"Those who never learn that compassion means to suffer with and not for another; end up living their lives as victims. If they're not sabotaging their own lives, they're harming ours. Empty from the loss of self and at the mercy of their needs, they grope in the dark. The dream text implies they become deformed, while our language today would say they are emotionally maladjusted."

"And, remember," I said. "They eventually become maladjusted adults. Such a beginning leaves them vulnerable to seek nourishment elsewhere. This is how we get stuck seeking comfort in the base elements – sex, drugs, work – and we flock to it in despair."

"Yes," agreed Rabbi Marish. "Living in the driest place internally, people find pleasure in their suffering and become addicted to the emotions that accompany it. They are naïve to the effects of the darkest of human qualities and hide them from the outside world."

"Wow!" I said. "This is sounding more and more like what happened to Job. His defense was collapsing and, overwhelmed, he lost the desire to fight."

Pieta nodded. "Our life and all of its richness can evaporate into a cloud of anxiety. The ego does not stop the human tendency for consumption, and when this addiction to our fear overtakes us, we ARE in despair."

"Ironically, the key distortion in the culture about compassion is that while human beings weep for the less fortunate, the soul is weeping for all those who lack self-love," the rabbi said. "We know that suffering has been useless when we feel that because we've suffered, we feel entitled. When that happens, the heart is stuck in a grieving process and needs to heal."

"Wait," I said. "We began this discussion again after hearing about the Kaddish. Help me understand what the Kaddish has to do with our dream text."

"Remember," the rabbi answered, "the Kaddish prayer is an act of loving-kindness toward a departed soul, enabling the soul to ascend to a higher realm. And, it has been well-noted that the Kaddish is the echo of Job in the prayer book: 'Though He slays me, yet will I trust in Him.'"

"Yes, yes," Pieta answered, "but in the context of the dream, Job is experiencing a great loss while questioning faith in his choices, correct?"

"Yes," he answered. "Job is trying to resolve his lapse in faith by seeking answers to these questions: What part of us is ego and what part is divine inheritance? Is it a mistake to follow one's heart because its passion can be overwhelming? In the end, he learns that mercy, or letting go of his fear internally, causes him to evolve."

"Yes!" Pieta added excitedly. "We are all trained to fear the ego and the over-whelming emotions that accompany it. And, yes its guilt is hard to bear. So, he learns to respect and understand his fears rather than worship them."

"Yes, divinity is celebrated in the heart," the rabbi continued. "Observing, witnessing, and understanding the relationship between the heart and ego is our burden of proof. Once we have it, we can wear it with pride and offer its message to the world."

"Ah," I said. "I get it. Rather than submitting to the fear of the ego, Job is attempting to trust his heart, and this requires faith?"

"Exactly!' the rabbi answered. "The Kaddish is a vigorous declaration of faith. It is one of the most beautiful, deeply significant, and spiritually moving prayers in the Jewish liturgy. It is a call to God from the depths of catastrophe, exalting His name and praising Him, despite the realization that He has just wrenched a human being from life."

"And," Pieta added, "we also know that in the context of this dream, it is a call to the higher self, after an internal struggle that resulted in his revelation and transformation."

The Astonishing Dream of JOB

"Meaning Job underwent a psychic or egoic death?" I asked.

"Yes," the rabbi answered. "A death we all have to endure to wake up to who we really are."

As the evening came to a close, Pieta and I were humbled and dizzy about the correlations and connections we'd seen today. We were sensing that the end of our quest was near, and we wondered what the rabbi had in store for us tomorrow. Most of the congregation had walked one by one to the back of the room to exit. As everyone was leaving, the rabbi rearranged the chairs while he watched. We could hear the people milling around outside.

"Go on," he said. "Go outside, get some air, and see what's going on. I will be there in a second."

As Pieta and I exited, a couple was nestled together, lying in the soft grass. The normally docile streets of Safed were buzzing with activity as a small street fair was just ending. We could see off in the distance where couples, families, and friends had littered the nearby street sharing food, drink, and good times. As my eyes lifted upwards to the darkening sky, the air brimmed with anticipation. What a glorious end to such an eventful day.

"Seems you may have missed some excitement," the rabbi said, exiting the synagogue. "The small street fairs here are something else."

"That's okay," I said. "I wouldn't have traded today's conversation for anything."

"Yes, yes," Pieta added. "Your contribution today answered so many of our questions. Thank you so much."

"Not to mention," I continued, "supporting many of our own conclusions about compassion and suffering."

"You are very welcome," the rabbi said as his gaze rested on the night sky. "And we've been blessed with a beautiful night."

"Indeed," Pieta said. There was a mutual silence as everyone sighed into the moment.

"Well," the rabbi said, "enjoy the evening. I need to get home to my wife. Be safe and I will see you tomorrow. I have someone I want you to meet."

Shaking his hand and saying our goodbyes, Pieta and I watched as the rabbi walked toward his house pulling his cloak around him. The evening air was beginning to chill.

"Amazing," Pieta sighed, his face glowing in contentment as I nodded in agreement.

"Yeah," I replied. "What an end to a glorious day. Let's see if any of these street vendors are still serving food."

The whole sky was illuminated with the setting sun as we walked toward the fair. We were both going to sleep well tonight.

The Astonishing Dream of JOB

The Human Spark

8

Spiritual Truths

71. Honor the heart's intelligence but also know the ego's first secret; fear.

72. Resolving fear means unlocking and understanding the unconscious.

73. Inside our darkest fears is our divine truth.

74. The human spirit does not know "the way" but it provokes the ego "along the way."

75. The human spark is proof of our divine connection – to everything.

76. Wisdom comes from "suffering with" the ego's fears, not suffering for them.

77. Understanding comes from avoiding anything that magnifies fear.

78. The ego's second secret: it can only see our lives two-dimensionally.

79. The human heart sees the "whole" of our life and views it three-dimensionally.

80. Knowing the relationship between heart and ego is our burden of proof. Worn with pride we can offer its message to the world.

The Astonishing Dream of JOB

9

Kept in the Dark

We were awakened by a delivery to Pieta from Hadi, the artifacts dealer. Rabbi Marish arrived shortly after as promised, reminding us of today's planned introductions. It turned out that Pieta had privately asked Hadi the night we were together to look for a codex on the black market that would help his mentor make sense of the final portion of the dream. Now, as the codex arrived, he told me it was a necessary manual to have to give us closure about Job's experience. Pieta was ecstatic about the arrival of the package, knowing his mentor at home would be pleased. As it turned out, Hadi's codex was the missing piece we had been searching for all along.

Once Pieta had opened the package and spent some time with it, he showed me the book. It was bound leaves of paper, or parchment, and appeared to be a rough copy of symbols and related notes.

"By the first century A.D. these manuals were used for commercial copies of classical literature," Pieta explained. "Early Christians adopted this parchment manual format for the scriptures used in their liturgy because a codex was easier to handle than a scroll. These symbol interpretations will help my mentor greatly."

Rabbi Marish interrupted and told us that he thought we should meet a man named Pastor Roker who lived in Safed.

"Pastor Roker has seen the portion of the dream that deals with Job's guilt and anger," he said. "Not only that, he seems to have a vantage point on its understanding, spiritually, that I agree with. I don't agree with his agenda, but that doesn't preclude you two from meeting him."

"What's his agenda?" I asked.

Rabbi Marish told us that Pastor Roker was a Messianic Jew, which we later found out really meant that he was a Christian Jew.

"The vast majority of Messianics worldwide are Christian, and only a tiny minority is really Jewish," the rabbi explained. For some reason these Christian Messianics have a strong desire to belong to the Jewish people. Many people consider their actions hostile because they want to missionize the Jews."

"Missionize the Jews?" I asked. "What does that mean exactly?"

"It is when Christian missionaries learn from the Jews. They participate in sacred meals, go to synagogue, and attend Jewish lectures. Once they have learned whatever they've needed to learn or absorb, they start missionizing Jews. They advocate that you can be Jewish and still believe in a messiah."

"Ahhhh," I said, understanding who these people were. "I can see where that would be highly controversial."

Pieta shook his head.

"Why would someone claim false Jewishness?" he asked.

"Some people simply want to be close to their Messiah, while others want to belong to the chosen people," the rabbi said.

***

Pastor Roker lived in a second-floor apartment on Canaan Street. There was a bomb shelter down a block, too far to reach, I noted, in the seven to ten seconds of warning a person would have once the air-raid sirens sounded. He lived in a section of Safed that was no stranger to rocket fire.

Once we arrived, Rabbi Marish introduced us to Pastor Roker. But before we could settle in, Pastor Roker decided he wanted to show us the shelter.

Out on the street, residents sitting in the sunlight across the street from the apartment seemed to be enjoying a day of calm. Pastor Roker told us they were waiting for a representative from the city to bring them a shopping bag of food, toys, and books.

"You can go insane in these shelters if you have to stay in them for very long," he said. "It's even worse if you have children. There is nothing for them to do."

He took us to an underground, windowless room with harsh lighting and three mattresses.

"We're excited, however, because the city just put in an air conditioner," he said.

A toddler in the shelter clutched a new puzzle and a Hebrew translation of a popular nursery book. Another youngster, maybe about nine or ten years old, took Pieta's hand leading him outside to show him two houses down the street that recently had been hit by rocket fire. Though he had a strong local accent, his English was surprisingly good.

"See," said the boy, whose name was Baruch, He pointed to the construction in front of a one-family house. "There

The Astonishing Dream of JOB

used to be a two-car garage there. Now they are rebuilding it."

He kicked the dust under the porch of his apartment building with his tennis shoe. Three teenagers were sitting in the house rubble smoking.

"The booms are really scary," said Baruch. "The last time they came, I didn't want to leave the bomb shelter at all. My mother coaxed me out with the promise of a bicycle."

We were enthralled with this little boy and his story. Pieta chatted with him a few minutes longer, then Pastor Roker gestured us out the door and we followed him back to his apartment.

"My wife and I have lived on faith for twenty-eight years," the pastor explained. "And each morning we wake up with expectancy about what God will surprise us with. It is the expectancy of prophecy. We have faith that such revelations of divine will or predictions of the future will occur. We have already seen how prophecy is gradually being revealed in Israel."

As we sat on the upstairs porch of his apartment, Pastor Roker offered us tea. The evening sun was slipping behind the buildings and the heat of the day was subsiding. Rabbi Marish sipped his drink as Pieta began the discussion.

"Does it bother you that this rewritten version of Job is surfacing, or that it is tampering with the text of the Bible?" Pieta asked.

"In a way, the fact that we can't prove dreams such as these testifies to the enduring presence of Divinity in the human condition," he answered. "…doesn't matter. Whether such information in dreams is ancient or comes from modern men or women—Jew or non-Jew alike—this dream text is a living testament to the author's desire for us to understand that Job's experience is universal in the human condition."

"Meaning that the author of the dream interpretation wanted us to understand what Job was experiencing internally?" I asked for clarification.

"Yes," the rabbi interjected. "Dreams come from secret places and connect us to the legacy of mystery. They perplex us, discomfort us. They are meaningless, yet saturated with meaning; alien, yet totally familiar; disturbing and still a consolation. It is hard to ignore something this intriguing."

"And," I added, "Job begged that someone write down his experience."

"So, you have seen the specific portion of the dream text where Job is questioning his own indignation?" Pieta asks. "He's feeling guilty even though he knows in his heart that questioning what is happening to him is somehow unfair?"

"Yes," the pastor answered. "He is questioning whether the emotion of anger is more ethical than the ego. In fact, he is seeking a solution for what he is feeling."

"Interestingly," said the rabbi, "the dream confirms that he is storing his anger, anxiety, and fear in his stomach. He wonders if it is guilt. The dream text specifically prescribes a practice of shallow but deep breathing so that his anger can be released."

"Amazing!" I said. "The dream is offering meditative advice. Where is the anger coming from?"

"That's easy," said Pieta. "We've learned so far that it's happening because he wants to trust his heart over the ego."

"Remember," said the Rabbi, "the spiritual sequence is that the human spirit/spark provokes the ego into action, which then causes an emotional reaction. The question, will it be the 'right' action, is based solely on the ego's judgments.

The Astonishing Dream of JOB

Job contends that including the heart in the equation assures that we will make the ethical choice."

"The heart is our compass then?" I asked.

"Yes," the rabbi answered, "especially when it comes to the spiritual freedom to be who we are."

"The goal then is not egoic perfection?" Pieta asks. "It is to stay connected to our personal truth?"

"Yes!" the rabbi said, smiling.

Pastor Roker beckoned for his wife to bring us more tea and asked if we were hungry. Pieta tilted his glass for a refill.

"The message here is that an ego awake uses discernment as a form of instruction not unlike constructive criticism, or people playing devil's advocate. Asleep, this same ego attacks and judges the self and others," the pastor said.

"Yes, Yes!" I said. "We've learned that the spirit provokes the ego for us to suffer with ourselves until we awaken to our heart's guidance. Not the other way around."

"Yes," he continued. "The dream suggests one in one thousand can do what is ethical without being provoked, or instructed, into consciousness. Said differently, one in one thousand is actually connected to their hearts."

"Yes, I said. "And I am taken with how that statistic is even more significant today with billions of people on the planet. No wonder so many of us feel like victims, we're all suffering for ourselves but unconscious about how to do it differently."

"Yes," he answered. "And the implication is that suffering with the ego is three times faster than waiting for you to simply get it along the path of life."

"What does that mean?" Pieta asked.

"Though many of us feel that we can never fully please the ego," he answered, "there is a great spiritual distance between a maturing ego and compassion. This distance is negotiated by doing the work of self-discovery, which is rewarded in the end by enlightenment and the freedom to be."

"Yes," the rabbi adds. "And, the message here is that we will not be spiritually awakened unless forced into awareness by the ego's judgments."

"It is even deeper than that," the pastor replied. "The dream suggests that Job knows the hypocrisy that mankind is capable of, so we are kept in the dark until we take responsibility for this. We can potentially create incredible things, but at the same time cause great atrocities."

"Does this mean that a spiritually mature person surrenders to their heart's guidance?" Pieta asked. "It doesn't just happen naturally?"

"Exactly!" the pastor answered. "In this context, an ego awake guides us to surrender, while an ego asleep simply defends and judges. Out of this evolves our tendency to use our creations to destroy."

"And people who judge," I added, "judge all the time, twenty-four-seven. And, when they are not judging themselves, they're judging others."

"Yes," the rabbi agreed. "And there is no compassion in that."

"In this context," the pastor continued, "we get the sense that Job is the first gifted compassionate because he does have a close relationship with his own suffering. He is deeply aware that he is not faking the heart's ethic. This is why he feels the ego's abuse is unnecessary and undeserving."

"He was already practicing the golden rule before it was written," Pieta said.

The Astonishing Dream of JOB

The pastor smiles.

"Are you familiar with Rabbi Isaac of Akko?" the pastor asked.

"We have heard about him some in our travels," I answered.

"Well, he taught that in order to have tranquility throughout your life, you must adhere to three things and distance yourself from the opposite. If you do, he suggested, you will have peace, not only in this lifetime, but also afterward."

"What are the three things?" I asked.

"Find satisfaction with your portion, love solitude, and remain free from arrogance and self-importance."

"You feel that this is the source of Job's upset?" Pieta asked. "He felt he was living his life as intended until the interruption and tragedy of this storm?"

"Absolutely!" the pastor answered. "And thanks to the dream's account of his reaction, we get to imagine pieces of a spiritual crisis that may have predated Christ. I am deeply moved by that. Like I said before, dreams may not be verifiable but they do testify to the enduring presence of Divinity in the human condition."

"Oh yes," Pieta answered. "It has so much meaning at this time in our history. More and more people are struggling to wake up to a meaningful life and are stuck or confused. My concern is that these profound messages will be resisted because they challenge the Bible."

"Our purpose here is only to understand," the pastor said. "We do not want to put down any personal beliefs or values. All open-minded people should try to follow the truth when it becomes clear to them."

"Are you not concerned that these messages will be resisted among Christians?" I asked.

"As far as the ancient manuscripts of the Bible are concerned, biblical scholars know that most of the manuscripts came from the fourth century C.E. and later. The manuscripts that are discovered are mostly partial and their texts differ from each other considerably," the pastor said.

"The New Testament is now known in whole or in part in nearly five thousand Greek manuscripts alone," the rabbi added. "Every one of those handwritten copies differs from the other one. It has been estimated that those manuscripts and quotations differ among themselves between 150,000 and 250,000 times. The actual figure is perhaps much higher."

"In fact," the pastor continued, "a study of 150 Greek manuscripts of the Gospel of Luke revealed more than 30,000 different readings. It is safe to say that there is not one sentence in the New Testament that is wholly uniform."

The pastor paused to refill his glass with tea. "Has anyone recently seen a Good News Bible?" the pastor asked.

"One was on our end table in one of our hotel rooms since we've been here," Pieta answered.

"Well," the pastor continued, "you can see for yourself that in the 1,300 pages of this modern English version, there are many footnotes pointing to phrases, sentences, and passages that are omitted or added by various ancient manuscripts or versions. Many of these alterations are not unintentional scribal errors such as you'd expect to see in handwritten copies of a book. A careful study of ancient texts has convinced scholars that the variations found in them were intentional tampering with the texts."

The Astonishing Dream of JOB

Pieta suddenly smiled. "So your answer is that you're not concerned about the text being found!" Pieta exclaimed. "This deeper version of Job's experience will be received with an open mind by those who have the capacity to see its worth."

Rabbi Marish and Pastor Roker both nodded. "Those of us in this work know that Bible tampering is still going on for various political and ideological reasons," the rabbi said.

"How so?" I asked.

"For example, under the pressure of Jewish organizations," he answered, "many churches in America and Europe have begun rephrasing Jesus's criticism of the Jews in the Gospels. Feminist groups are urging the use of unisex language in the new versions. Homosexual groups have their own versions. All these changes are taking place before our own eyes."

"You know," I said, "this is not something one would think is happening unless they were engaged in this kind of dialogue."

"That's it, isn't it?" said the rabbi. "We are all excited that this version of Job's experience will open new dialogue about how to be more compassionate human beings. How can that not be a blessing?"

"So then, self-condemnation or criticism can be a good thing?" Pieta asked.

"The dream implies that you have a vertical relationship with the Divine," the pastor answered. "Yes, self-criticism can be a good thing if one has merged the heart's intelligence with the ego's discernment. This is what Eastern philosophy calls mindfulness."

"The dream points out that the mere number of victims in the world that complain and want revenge is overwhelming," the rabbi added. "Most of us are in our heads."

"Ego that is guided by the heart is fair?" Pieta asked.

"It is," the pastor answered. "Egos do not lie or reject—we do! Ego simply mirrors what we have been taught. Unlearning these conditioned behaviors and altering our initial programming is our challenge."

"If people witness and observe their lives daily from the neutral perspective of the heart," added the rabbi, "they will be happy. If they do not, they are at the mercy of self-judgment. The dream text explains that complainers and manipulators are evidence of those immersed in such judgments."

Pieta got up to stretch, as we had been sitting for a long time. As he returned, he smiled at Pastor Roker and picked up where we'd left off.

"I heard once," Pieta said, "that 'crazy' is you or me amplified. We really need to pay attention to how the ego makes us feel."

"Yes," I said. "We are amplifying our thinking with our emotions, instead of feeling our way through them."

"The text suggests that the ego presents as an inner noise, and the volume can be overwhelming. And often it comes without warning," said Rabbi Marish.

"Most of us are so intimidated by this noise that we do unimaginable things to make it stop or to distract ourselves," I added.

"This is true," the rabbi said. "Out of this amplified thinking we are covertly introduced to the human shadow."

"This is the source of Job's inner storm, isn't it?" Pieta asked. "It is actually a storm of emotions brought on by fear and doubt?"

The Astonishing Dream of JOB

"Yes," answered Pastor Roker. "An ego awake would command that we figure this out. It questions: Do we have the strength and courage to know what it knows when we are emotionally upset? Because of the heart's guidance, it knows the difference between being conscious or asleep."

Pieta nodded. "How can we possibly complain when we are consumed in our shadows? What will guide us if not these constructive criticisms from an ego awake?"

"Again," I said, "an ego awake or conscious uses the heart as a compass, yes?"

"Yes," the pastor continued. "Job is teaching us that this emotional storm can be pretty cold without feeling the heart's warmth or guidance. The text suggests that coldness comes from our thinking and fear from an unconscious ego."

As the pastor spoke, I noticed Pieta looking at his watch. Rabbi Marish was also beginning to show the fatigue of the day. We knew that our time in Safed was limited, and we were anxious to have a little time to sightsee. After we thanked Pastor Roker and Rabbi Marish for their gracious contributions to our search, Pieta asked them about the city.

"I'm sure you have noticed that all of Safed is built in a circular fashion on a hilltop," the rabbi said. "There are local buses and unofficial cabs that will take you about the town."

We thanked Pastor Roker and Rabbi Marish again for their time and decided to spend the rest of our evening processing what they had shared with us over dinner. We were also looking forward to losing ourselves in the beauty and mystical ambiance of this ancient town.

9
Spiritual Truths

81. We are in truth being pushed toward consciousness.

82. 'Right' action is ego and the moral choice—'context' is heart and the ethical choice.

83. An ego awake uses discernment to instruct constructively—asleep, this same ego attacks and judges.

84. The human spirit provokes ego to suffer with itself to awaken to the heart's guidance.

85. One in one thousand of us are ethical without being provoked into consciousness.

86. Suffering with the ego is three times faster than waiting to get it or awaken by chance.

87. There is great spiritual distance between a maturing ego and compassion. This is decreased by self-recovery.

88. We are kept in the dark until we take responsibility for faking this maturity.

89. Spiritual maturity is surrendering to the heart's guidance.

90. An ego awake guides us to surrender—an ego asleep defends its ignorance.

The Astonishing Dream of JOB

10

The Answer to Why

I was jarred awake by the sound of the phone ringing. It was Pieta's mentor calling from the United States to tell him that Bible literalists were heating up over the attention being given the dream text. Since Bible literalists do not believe anything in the Bible is symbolic, they were up in arms over the dream text being made public, and they wanted to know who was responsible for bringing it to light. Once Pieta got off the phone with his mentor, he told me that the fundamentalists and evangelicals were worked up and that we were going to need to be careful about who we talked to as we moved forward on our journey.

Pieta relayed what is mentor had said: "Some experts are responding with a mixture of caution, hope, and skepticism to claims that this recently discovered dream text may shed some light on our earlier spiritual development. That is certainly my hope. To make any claims right now about the spiritual value of this document may be a bit reckless."

In that moment of sharing, I realized for the first time that Pieta's mentor had the full text, and I expressed my surprise.

"Yes," Pieta answered. "He has it, but the final pages are written in code. We need to crack the code and decipher what's on those final pages. Getting him the codex has to be our top priority. There is likely to be considerable academic and political debate about the text's authenticity, meaning, and interpretation. But for now, there is a race against time to safeguard the document's future. We have no time to spare."

"Why didn't you tell me your mentor had the whole text?"

Looking at me with a frown, Pieta lowered his head to speak. "I hope you are not angry with me. But this entire quest has been about getting this codex."

"Why all the secrecy?" I asked.

Pieta looked uncomfortable. "I am sorry my friend," he replied. "My mentor is a very private person, and acknowledging that he has possession of this document will force him into public view. He is laboring over that possibility."

Pieta shared that he feared we might have been on a wild goose chase and he felt concerned that I'd be mad if I found out. Had it not been for meeting Hadi, he confessed, he wasn't sure the trip would have been worth it.

"I trust you," I told him. "No need to apologize. You have never disappointed me as a mentor or as a friend. This journey with you has been incredible."

Pieta and I had been warned early on in our quest, by Zoe, that there would be zealots capable of stirring things up back in the States, especially those who would see the interpretation as tampering with the Bible. But it was still difficult to imagine that these people would publicly condemn the text without hearing its depth and what it had to offer. But the phone call from Pieta's mentor certainly validated Zoe's claims.

"So far as I can tell," I said, "the dream text doesn't contain any significant difference from other wisdom teachings about human suffering."

"True," Pieta answered. "And, it allows spiritual seekers from around the world to witness the process of self-recovery and awakening, a necessary piece for all those uninspired by the current teachings of George Gurdjieff, A.H. Almaas, Poonja, Gangaji, Rudolf Steiner, Eckhart Tolle, and Byron Katie, to mention a few."

"How can we not be moved?" I asked. "It's an astonishing document that answers contemporary questions about the why of human suffering."

"Yes," Pieta continued. "Maybe the conservatives fear that this text is saying something that is in conflict with their beliefs when, in fact, it does not."

"Maybe," I said.

"We have to be prepared to enter a storm of controversy when we get back to the States," Pieta told me.

"I am ready," I said. This adventure had already shed light on my personal convictions, and I was ready to stand by Pieta and his mentor all the way until the end.

***

The next morning, Pieta called Pastor Roker's home and spoke to his wife. She told him he was busy and would have to call us back. We asked if we could send him a copy of the fax sent by Pieta's mentor of the newspaper articles.

Next Pieta called Rabbi Rabino, a friend of Rabbi Marish, and asked to meet with him. All we knew for sure was that he, too, had questions about the text. He agreed to see us that evening.

The Astonishing Dream of JOB

As soon as Pieta hung up, the phone rang. It was Pastor Roker calling us back. Pieta put him on speaker phone and he started in.

"First of all, let me say that the word is out that you and your friend are asking questions about the dream text. My wife tells me that you are communicating with someone in the States who is concerned about the fundamentalist reaction to the text. Is this because he has it?" Roker asked.

Pieta confirmed his suspicions and shared the nature of his relationship with his trusted friend in the States.

"Well," Pastor Roker continued, "I am certain that no one will talk to you now that this has been made public. Knowledge of your search has traveled fast. Also, the local news is broadcasting the fundamentalist reaction to the text in the States."

"Why would anyone refuse to talk to us?" Pieta asked.

"Many of the Jewish groups here abhor Christian evangelicals," he answered. "And, there is a political division between the groups. The Orthodox and Conservatives welcome evangelical support, while Reform and secular ones oppose it."

"So, you're saying that the people we want to talk to are political liberals who would refuse to talk to us because they don't want to get involved with anything having to do with Christian fundamentalists," Pieta asked.

"Yes," he replied.

"I see," I said. "Because the local Jews believe that the United States was founded as a Christian nation, and, since they worry about the decay of morality, they wish to impose a conservative moral code."

"Exactly!" Pastor Roker said. "The liberals here will shy away from this conversation now that the conservatives are involved."

"Maybe so," Pieta answered. "But we just made a meeting with Rabbi Rabino."

"All I can tell you," Pastor Roker replied, "is that once every one hears about the potential of being attacked for their liberal support of this text, they will withdraw their invitation to speak with you. Mark my words."

Within an hour of hanging up with Pastor Roker, Rabbi Rabino called to cancel his meeting with us. As Pastor Roker predicted, he did not want to bring attention to himself.

"I am sorry," he said. "I fear that you may use my words out of context and somehow make me a target. I am not as informed as some of the other teachers. You might want to try to meet with them."

"No one else is willing to talk to us," Pieta answered.

"There are other local and liberal spiritual teachers who might speak if you come to them in secret, and if you promise to not use their names as supporters of the dream's discovery," he replied.

Despite our pleading, the rabbi refused to meet with us. Our last contact was to be another acquaintance of Rabbi Marish. Although Pastor Roker had made it clear that no one would be willing to speak with us further, Pieta did not want to take his word for it and made efforts to contact Rabbi Cooper. He left a message with the rabbi's wife, but she refused to take down our phone number, saying that her husband did not return phone calls. Despite many attempts, we were unable to reach him. We had to accept the truth: between the local news about what was happening in the States and our motives becoming known, we had lost all privileges to meet or speak with local spiritual teachers. We stopped by to give our farewells to Rabbi Marish and to express our gratitude for his contribution to our search. Pieta used his phone to call his mentor in the States.

"It seems our time over here is finished," he said. "Has the situation calmed at home since we spoke last?"

Although I could not hear the conversation, I could tell Pieta was relieved by his mentor's answer. We would be returning home soon.

***

Typical of the summers in Safed, the days began very hot and humid. It had been three days since Pastor Roker warned us we had lost our anonymity. This became even more evident when we began receiving phone calls from people we had met along our journey.

"We are hearing that local teachers are refusing to speak to you now," Zoe said. "Did you get what you came for?"

We learned from Zoe that someone had sent an email to the Rabbi in Akko. Word of the fundamentalist reaction in the States was causing a knee-jerk hesitation from the higher ups in Israel. Technology and a tight-knit group of rabbis were quickly spreading the news about what was happening—including our involvement.

"We got plenty of feedback," Pieta told her, "and we found the codex my mentor needed. Our journey here has been a great success."

"You are wonderful people," Zoe said. "Be safe as you return home."

As we readied ourselves to travel back to the States, Pieta called his mentor one last time. He told Pieta that the national media had been interviewing a few prominent conservatives in the States, but he was less concerned about what was happening than he had been last time they spoke.

Answer to Why

Pieta told me that we were going to return home and go straight to see his mentor. It was obvious that the final chapter of our journey, as well as the epilogue to Job's experience, was going to come directly from the person who had the entire dream.

"That will be exciting," I said. "The codex gives your mentor the piece he needs to summarize his discovery. Is he feeling better about how public it's become?"

"Yes, his focus is on finding the truth in this ancient document. If that means having to go public, I believe he will do it," he answered. "In my opinion, it's a window of publicity that will spread the dream's message faster. I respect my mentor's spiritual honesty and integrity approaching a find of this magnitude. But, he knows that timing its release is important too."

***

It had been two weeks and a day since we first landed in Israel, but it seemed much longer. We awoke the following morning at 4:30 a.m. to catch our flight home. En route to the airport, Pieta and I rode in silence in the taxi. We were still absorbing what was happening. Having landed in Jericho, Damascus International surprised us. The terminal appeared new and it was much bigger than we expected.

Our conversation on the plane was minimal. We were both lost in our thoughts about what was going to happen once we got home. Thankfully, we had only one connecting flight, and it didn't seem as long as I had anticipated. Before I knew it, we were back in Pieta's car and on our way to his mentor's home. "What are you thinking about?" I asked to break the silence.

Without taking his eyes off the road, Pieta replied, "I'm a little nervous about what is in store for my mentor. He has been retired and become reclusive of late. He certainly has a lot at stake with this." As Pieta expounded about his mentors upcoming lost anonymity, my mind went to the profound teachings we had heard so far: that the heart IS our ethical compass; that the ego needs to be provoked into action; that our spiritual journey is to understand the nature of our fears.

"I guess I fear that in the end the text will be suppressed," I said. "So many of us live our lives and never know why things are as they are. We never get answers to profound questions about our meaning and purpose. I want to become one of the one in one thousand who teaches the others about this text."

"Yes," Pieta said. "That is an admirable goal. And our journey with this text is far from over. We've made an important contribution to this discovery."

My stomach drew into a knot with this realization. "I see why you didn't want to tell me initially. I would have felt responsible if we had not been able to complete our quest."

"Yes, I know," he said. "I was trying to spare you that worry. In addition to making sense of Job's experience, my mentor has to be convinced that this discovery will raise humanity's consciousness. I know, like Job, he wanted to trust his intuition based on what he understood about the text thus far."

We rode in silence again, the countryside becoming darker as the sun set behind us. My mind went over all that had happened since Pieta met me at the lodge weeks earlier. My life path had been confirmed. I was, and always had been, connected to my inner compass. Like Job, I was convinced of an inner truth different than what I was experiencing. I knew this now. The truths of spiritual recovery discovered in this reinterpretation of an ancient text affirmed and answered so many questions about my own healing. I had studied human development and personality dynamics my entire career, but nothing I had ever read explained the ego's true function as well as this ancient text did. Nothing merged the concepts of mind, body, soul, and spirit any better. Everything that we had heard during our journey about how and why people suffer was the missing piece our culture needed to promote deeper understanding and healing. I knew that we were about to reveal something that would assist a necessary shift in many people's lives.

When we were just a few miles from his mentor's home, Pieta broke the silence. "Remember," he said, "my mentor's solitude and privacy are very important to him. He is totally entrenched in his spiritual work. Don't be surprised if he is brusque with you. We might need to carefully coax him to reveal and share these teachings. I need you to follow my lead."

Although it was almost dark, the countryside was still overwhelmingly beautiful. We were approaching a piece of paradise ahead, a log cabin situated at the center of this secluded plot of land. The evening silence was broken by barking. As we approached, our headlights revealed two excitable dogs that began jumping on the sides of our truck as soon as we pulled to a stop. In the frame of the front door appeared a silhouette of a man. He was of average build, but as we walked toward him, there was nothing average about his expression. There was a calm and certainty in his face that would put anyone at ease.

"Come in! Come in!" he said, gesturing. "We have a lot to discuss."

Pieta turned to me and introduced us, "This is my friend and mentor, Dr. Richard McCauley. We have known each other for forty years."

Taking his hand in mine, he gave me what was not a typical handshake. There was no force in his grip, just a comfortable and safe greeting.

The Astonishing Dream of JOB

"It is nice to meet you," he said. "I imagine you are both glad to be home, especially given the climate in Safed."

"Yes, after the word spread that the conservatives were unhappy with the dream's message it was like we were lepers," Pieta said. "No one wanted to draw attention to themselves. Are you feeling better about the news coverage?"

"Honestly," he said, "I am not sure how to feel. This is bringing me out of hiding in a way that I guess was inevitable, but still, my ego is resisting it."

"I think this will help you," Pieta said, handing him the codex.

"Oh yes," he said. "This IS exciting."

"Can we see the dream interpretation?" Pieta asked. "All we have left to understand in the story is where God's voice comes from the whirlwind. We want to see how the author of the dream handles this."

"Yes, of course," Richard said. "But first, I want to thank you for your patience with me. I wanted to share more, but I felt it more important for you to stay focused on finding the codex. I needed you to experience the truths gradually and profoundly. I knew if you did that, you would be able to embrace the text's conclusion later."

"You make it sound like it's going to be difficult," I said.

"Well, as you know," Richard answered, "much of what is revealed about the dream text thus far offers us an answer to why suffering happens as it does. In contrast, the theological study of the Book of Job has been about how to suffer, and even this is incomplete."

I felt like Richard was about to uncover something important. "So, why do we suffer?" I asked excitedly.

"First, let's remember the sequence of the experience," Richard said. "We come into the world with a divine connection, and it is evidenced as the human spark. Its function, through the human spirit, is to provoke the developing ego into action. Born free-spirited, we have to acquire a sense of right and wrong. While we spend time externally learning the rules, internally there may or may not be a developing ethic. The compass for this ethic is the human heart. Unless we are conscious, we do not know this. Suffering provides the impetus for us to surrender to this knowing."

I nodded. "We are an ego asleep that has to be pushed into an ego awake."

"Exactly," he answered. "Remember, Job asks in the beginning: 'My heart has never lied to me, why should I listen to the ego?' The implication here is that he believed in the heart but did not know it. Surrendering through suffering is the path to this ethical knowledge."

"What is the teaching regarding why humans suffer?" Pieta asked.

"The ego is our foundation," Richard answered. "It is where and how we start. It helps us form and realize our dreams. Provoked by the human spirit and orchestrated by the soul, it creates rites of passage for us to live in the present. In essence, the fear of its judgments motivates us."

"Why fear and not love?" Pieta asked.

"Though we are born free, many of us are irresponsible with our freedom. This egoism or narcissism makes some believe we do not need love. Rather, we need control; hence, the fear. In fact, the dream text says that one in a thousand of us can possibly connect to our hearts. Job's experience demonstrates how to be the one."

"So, Job had to be awakened?" I asked.

The Astonishing Dream of JOB

"Yes," Richard answered. "His values, principles, and practices were not in question. Instead, it is the depth of his spiritual development. The implication is that people who learn through suffering are restored. Those who fake this character development are no more than slaves to their ego."

"This story about an inside experience to an outside event is absolutely amazing," I said. "It teaches us that spiritual maturity and development are processes that the meek do not choose."

"Yes, one needs to consider the spirit of his or her true self," Richard continued. "It begins the path to enlightenment. It reveals one's shadow, which, in this context, is an ego asleep or unconscious. Knowing the soul and spirit of something is all there is to know of anything. We can begin to answer questions like: 'Why am I here? What is my purpose? What has suffering taught me? Should I spread its teachings?'"

"There is no end to those kinds of questions, is there?" I mused.

"That is because people who choose to suffer the wilderness are not mere mortals," he answered. "They understand and grow from the void, or emptiness of their journey."

"I can't get past whom or what made this decision for us," I said. "According to Job's experience, by whose authority did fear become the dominant emotion in our culture?"

"The dream text suggests that WE are the authority, and this understanding will make a lot of people uncomfortable. We know that man is capable of unimaginable things—good and bad. Abandonment, loss, and rejection are cold realities of life that harden our emotions like stone, and then solidify what we would call personality or character."

"So, what we do with our suffering depends on how we will treat ourselves and each other?" I asked.

"Of course," he answered. "Melting this character through suffering is only possible if we are connected to our compass—the heart."

"In this context," Pieta said, "the ego is man's conscience?"

"Not only that, it is our conscience until we become conscious!" he answered.

"Wow!" I said. "That's an important distinction."

"Yes, pushed into consciousness through suffering and surrendering to the ethic of the heart, we are able to know our dreams, be grateful, realize our potential, share the wisdom of our journey, know why things are as they are, motivate others to seek a similar transformation, and teach people that they no longer have to be afraid."

"I have been dying to actually see the original document," Pieta said. "Can we read some of what you are talking about firsthand?"

I realized that I had goose bumps as Richard left the room to honor Pieta's request. The whole journey thus far had come to this moment. We were going to finally see the original reinterpretation of Job's experience.

Richard reentered with a large book. He told us that the paper the dream was written on was fragile. It was stored in between layers of special clear plastic sheets to insulate it from further exposure to the elements.

"Here is an example of a portion of the text that explains a function of ego," he said, opening the book. It reads: 'Ego offers a sanctuary in the desert and makes it possible to live there. The criticism of ego may prevent one from sensing that it is actually driving them. Awake they can use this motivation to work through life's trials. Asleep they will feel victim to the judgments. Those who trust the work reveal the seeds of their awakening and lay a natural foundation for their arrival.'"

"Wow!" I said. "This is making the distinction between an ego awake versus one asleep."

"Yes," he added. "There are many examples in the text that do this. Here is another," he said, turning the pages.

When the time comes to be free: ego will criticize your passion and its desire. Will you give strength to this passion or restrain it at the boundary of your thoughts and feelings for fear of judgment? Passion breaks ground with its choices and is proud as it prepares for the struggles of life. It dislikes fear but does not turn its back on challenge. Its companion is desire.

"This is beautiful," Pieta said. "You can see that these teachings are speaking to someone who is waking up to their potential. Passion is suffering, and once we are no longer afraid of it, we are propelled forward into our desires."

Richard nodded and then turned to another passage. "This portion addresses the anger we feel about our predicament."

Pursuing your passion asleep with anger can swallow your ground with no acknowledgment that an internal battle has begun. Awake, the ego will mock challenge, sense a battle is coming and encourage its beginning. Human potential grows from the blood of suffering: wherever it is available the spiritual will seek it.

"This is amazing," I said. "How can something this old and out of its original context be so accurate about spiritual recovery?"

"The implications are very profound and fits contemporary thought," he replied.

Answer to Why

"Where is the portion of the text that answers why Job had to suffer with himself?" Pieta asked.

Richard turned to another page. "Here is a section that deals with his transformation after questioning what has happened to him."

Knowing what you know now, would you stop the ego's judgments? Knowing what you know now, that the ego has two faces: asleep it can violently erupt with anger or aggression on one hand, but awake it can protect and nurture on the other? Knowing what you know now, that the heart is your compass but it has to be activated? Knowing what you know now, should you not rid yourself of your pride and righteous anger? Knowing what you know now, can you not see that every human being that is arrogant should be humbled? Understanding these things is proof that you have transformed into a knowing that now has the capacity to grow.

"I especially like this portion about the human shadow," Richard said. "We know, because of this text, that the shadow is an ego asleep. We witness this shadow as a personality that is detached from its heart and that has not been transformed by its suffering."

"Essentially, they are a victim of their own ignorance or naiveté?" Pieta asked.

"At least it is a kinder depiction than suggesting we are evil or possessed," Richard replied. "This is what it says."

Your nature, unaware and within the shadow, is secretly gestating. It is protected by the dark. Meanwhile your suffering and rebirth provide it direction. It can drink up the flow of life and not question: childlike it trusts that you will solve the problem of thirst. The ego holds this attribute captive until you become aware of it. Emotions alone cannot control your darkness nor restrict its self-expression. Will

The Astonishing Dream of JOB

you play with it because of its vulnerability or imprison it for your pleasure?

"This piece may be trying to enlighten us about addiction," I said. "What do you think?"

"It certainly implies that our darkness, when lost to simple survival, is waiting to be discovered. Our darkness is just repressed aspects of the self. If not attended to, this quality will look to satiate its desires. Addiction could be one result."

"Does the text tell us to take responsibility for these darker qualities?" Pieta asked.

"The entire text suggests that human suffering is built into our story to keep us humble," Richard replied. "Job might have been righteous, but he lacked a context or ethic for self-love. It turns out it is compassion—suffering with oneself by surrendering to what the heart knows. But Job initially spun into victim, suffering for himself, which is all about an ego asleep.

"Here is a piece of what the text says about being a victim," Richard continued.

Ego will not excite this dark power as it would be an act of cruelty. Nor does it spare anyone that complains about it. There is no other way to see behind the veil of fear and anger and its terrible effect in the world.

I took a deep breath and turned to Richard. "This suggests that we will not attack or condemn ourselves if we're awake, as this becomes a cruel re-enactment of our beginnings. That makes sense. We don't want to recreate our past wounds."

"Exactly," he answered. "We're all born unconscious and have to work our way into awareness. Although many of us complain about this predicament, we are given the ability for self-recovery and must set out on the road less traveled—willingly."

"This makes me think of The Wizard of Oz," I said, smiling. "We are all looking for our brain, heart, and courage. Only to find out in the end we already had it. And compassion is Dorothy, finding its way back home by imaging the choice."

"Yes," Richard answered. "The human spark is proof of our connection to the divine. In spite of what we go through on our journey, it remains safe inside of us. The catch is, we have to go in to find it. Only suffering throws us there."

Richard turned to another passage and read: 'Your true nature's self-worth and self-esteem is shielded from suffering, kept in place by experience upon experience. No outside influence can enter: each attribute sticking together holding the other fast so not to be separated. Once you know what you know now, you will also know the ease of joy. This inner healing is a glimmer of your passion, and its awareness the veil of awakening. Out of this expression comes a burst of the authentic self.'

'In this renewed version of the self: fear, anxiety and confusion become curiosity. Like something that has been percolating and brought to a boil, its influence ignites like coal and creates an assertive desire to self-express. Your strength comes from knowing the boundary between thoughts and feelings, as well as whatever your developing intuition may perceive.'

'Your inner life will heat up like a boiling pot, and produce a healing ointment. A shining trail of its journey will be left behind and represents the depth of the process. There is no power within the internal that can compare to this natural force that fears nothing. It sees everything from an above perspective and is the context that dictates or interferes with everyone's potential.'

The Astonishing Dream of JOB

"I know that once this dream text becomes public," Pieta said, "people will want to know over and over again why human beings have to suffer."

Using the codex to understand the remaining and final symbols, Richard's eyes darkened. We were on the brink of a life-defining moment and the energy in the room was palpable.

"It was as I suspected," he said. "I am a little uncomfortable with the answer Job discovers. It's a simple answer on one level, and deep on another. Either way, it's going to cause a stir. The answer to why we suffer is: Because!"

"What?!?" I exclaimed. "That can't be the answer. That's a parent's answer. Just Because? You are right—a lot of people will be upset if it's that simple."

"Oh, it's not simple," Richard replied. "First, 'Because' needs to be broken into two words. To 'Be' allows the real something else that follows—the authentic self that comes from a maturing ego now connected to the heart. We know now that recovering this aspect of the self requires us to surrender the unconscious ego as a useless victim so it can awaken to useful suffering, and then 'Cause' a meaningful, compassionate existence. Said differently, pay it forward."

"This was Job's argument then," I said. "He thought he was being himself when all hell broke loose."

"Yes," Richard answered. "But, he was unaware of his spiritual immaturity. He had to suffer to grow or suffer to become. Once he did this, the 'cause' would affect his life and the rest of the world."

"Why we suffer, answered as 'Because'." I said smiling. "Simple enough, but you are correct that it requires a second look to get the depth of the answer. If we truly be who we are intended to be, this causes an effect in the world?"

"Ahhh," Pieta said. "When Job held to his hearts knowing, it was a critical first step toward Becoming. Completing that process, he was considered the one in one thousand who could affect the other 999."

"Yes!" Richard replied.

"Wow!" I said. "And so, too, can we, right?"

"Though it is a path that only a select few choose, yes," Richard answered. "The text suggests that no single thought is hidden from the ego. The human challenge is to NOT believe the ego until you KNOW it."

"Ahhh," I said. "We must not just hear these inner voices, we need to see them."

"Yes, in our hearts and minds," Richard answered. "The soul communicates this to us through dream images or through our imagination. We know now if they are scary, it means our egos are asleep."

"This is the reason an ego awakened condemns the earlier self-talk?" Pieta asks. "Much of the inner guidance is initially about perfection and behaving a particular way."

"Absolutely," Richard answered. "In the end, the feeling self is accepted for its passion and its honesty, while moral righteousness is considered false. Rather than punish ourselves for these unconscious decisions, we are to show mercy."

"Which means to set ourselves free for the time spent serving the ego?" I asked. "We truly didn't know better, right? Many people still don't know."

We could hear the dogs barking outside. Someone was coming and we suddenly heard voices.

"He's in here. Hurry!" It was a camera crew from the local news.

The Astonishing Dream of JOB

Richard approached the door, shielding his eyes and face from the bright lights of a video camera and flashing bulbs. "Wait. Please wait," he said. "I will be out shortly. Please wait."

Richard shut the door and began moving through the house, closing all the curtains. The crew reluctantly pulled back and returned to their vehicles to wait, but several members lingered near the door in hopes of asking the first question.

I could see Pieta's concern for his mentor as Richard walked around the house securing the doors and windows. "I can only imagine what an invasion this must feel like for him," I said.

"Yes," Pieta replied. "He has given himself to people all of his life. He knows how consuming this is going to be."

Coming back into the living room having overheard what Pieta said, Richard responded, "It was inevitable my friends. While you were away, my old liberal colleagues were slowly leading the press to my door. I asked that they shield me as long as they could. It seems they've found me. The conservatives have been searching for the source of this information for weeks."

"Richard, please know how much we support you. Lou and I are greatly invested in this discovery, but you are our first concern."

"Thank you, Pieta," Richard replied. "I think we were all a little naïve to think we could keep the lid on something as special as this discovery, indefinitely."

Pieta sighed. "Those of us seeking to understand and publicly reveal this message simply want to help the human dilemma. We never consider the backlash. Lost anonymity seems a small price when you consider the benefit to the world.

Richard shrugged. "One of the things I knew when I invited you on this journey with me is that it was going to pull us both out of our comfort zones."

"Please Richard, before you address the press, what I asked before about people not knowing any better—do you agree?" I asked.

"Yes, Lou, we are naïve in the beginning," Richard replied. "The reward for awakening follows."

"How does the dream handle this?" Pieta asked. "In the Biblical Job story, his wife, children, and material possessions are restored over time."

"Yes, that's because after he makes an internal shift, mental perfection gives way to adaptability," Richard answered. "Synthesis becomes cooperation and harmony. Spontaneity for life is magnified. His ability to do and be in the world is improved. Qualities that initially fueled his questioning are now awakened and celebrated."

"The shift in consciousness that is supposed to be occurring in 2012—is it not mankind moving from Doing to Becoming?" Pieta asked.

"Yes," Richard replied. "The dream text suggests that these qualities did not exist before Job had his catharsis. In fact, they are now being discovered because of the spiritual journey of self-recovery then as well as now, thirty-six hundred years later!"

"So, what really happened when Job awakened?" I asked.

"In the context of the dream," Richard answered, "he imagined, because of his despair, that he was losing everything. Suffering himself awake, he realizes that nothing of the sort had happened. Instead, the experience fueled his catharsis. In that moment, he realized that everything looked brand new!"

The Astonishing Dream of JOB

"I see," Pieta said. "The type of world you perceive depends in large measure on the state of consciousness you are in. Most of us live with a painful sense of separation from others, a sense of something missing, and a pervasive feeling of limitation or fear."

"Exactly," Richard said. "Job was initially experiencing the illusion of separation. Once he awakened to the moment, he was whole again. And, as most of our contemporary spiritual teachers are saying, in the Now, everything is brand new."

Pieta and I were both so moved by this realization that we fell silent. Pieta was tearful. I was mesmerized by the words. Richard held an affirming smile. We all understood in that moment that this information was too valuable not to share. There was a softening of the resistance from Richard and he moved closer to the door.

We could hear the press clamoring for position on Richard's porch. Lights flickering, voices mumbling, our moment was coming soon.

"What do we know about the author of this dream?" I asked.

"The text," Richard answered, "is thought to be part of a collection of writings by a Jewish Mystic and Ethicist, Rabbi Isaac ben Samuel, of Akko. He lived in Akko in the twelfth century. But, I am sure this will be of great debate."

"Rabbi Marish spoke about him during our time with him," Pieta replied.

"Yes, of course," Richard answered. "He is little known today, but he had a deep influence on the development of the Kabbalah. He studied with the greatest Kabbalist thinkers of his time."

"Clearly he believed in the power of dreams," I said.

Answer to Why

"Rabbi Isaac aligned the Jewish ideals of meditative prayer with Islamic conceptions of prophecy, though the text is not affiliated with Islamic culture," Richard answered. "Prayer was considered a one-way path to God, with the person ascending to a high place to achieve the best communion with the Divine. According to Rabbi Isaac, however, meditative prayer could cause the mystic to draw down this power into the human soul, which would then be disseminated in the everyday world through prophetic actions."

"So, he believed that dreams performed the same function?" I asked.

"Yes, the specific energy that the prophetic mystic would utilize in his divinely ordained social role originated as the preexistent light of God. This Divine power was represented as an Essence that not only could be accessed, but also brought into the world through the dreams of the mystic."

"So, he is the author for sure?" I asked.

"That's going to be of some debate among theologians and historians, but it's not the most important question. I am just thrilled that the text exists in this form at all."

"Of course!" I concurred. "I am astonished by the statistic in the dream—that one in one thousand will be awakened. I wonder about its implications today?"

"It is a curious number, for sure," Pieta answered. "Do we know what the world's population was during Job's experience?"

"According to population experts," Richard answered, "it took almost nineteen hundred years for the world to slowly rise from an estimated 250 million at the time of Christ to 1.5 billion at the beginning of the twentieth century. Then, in the twentieth century alone, the earth's population has exploded, quadrupling in size. We are at the staggering mark of 7 billion people in the world today."

"I remember reading in the paper about the seventh billionth person being born." Pieta said. "It was October 31, 2011. I remember this because it coincided with a friend's birthday."

"Yes, I remember that, too," Richard replied. "Looking at all of this from a historic and prophetic point of view, crossing the seventh billion mark is more a cause for concern and alarm than for celebration."

"How so?" I asked.

"Well, according to the experts," he said, "it took 123 years to get from one billion to two billion people. Yet, it took only thirty-three years to reach the 3 billion mark and fourteen years to arrive at 4 billion."

"Wow!" I said. "That is scary."

"Yes, it becomes sobering when you look at such large numbers," Richard said. "Our present population will again double within fifty years."

"So, does the one in one thousand ratios of people who can cultivate this gift still apply?" Pieta asked.

"Yes, if we look at the United States, that statistic would mean that 300,000 of us have the capacity to awaken out of 300 million people," Richard answered. "What we are witnessing, though, is that the largest majority of those awakening are still serving the ego."

"The narcissism is still there, of course," I said.

"Yes," he said. "Remember, for a person to reconnect to his or her inner compass or heart, that person has to surrender. This means suffering with oneself voluntarily. What we are seeing in New Age spirituality is this concept that you can become conscious and make a million dollars.

Many are having wake-up moments, but in the end they are still an ego asleep.

"Suffering got their attention," I said. "But they were not humbled enough to get the deeper lesson."

"Exactly," he answered. "They are not connecting with their divinity. Instead, they are using the energy of the experience to sell the illusion of a shortcut to self-recovery."

"Whatever the statistic," Richard replied, "the urgency for the human race to wake up to its divine responsibility is upon us. This dream text provides a much-needed map and explains a process that is confusing for many."

Richard had no sooner said this than bright lights shone through the curtains in the living room where we stood. The press had returned, and this time they had created a crowd of onlookers. His isolated country road had turned into a one-lane traffic jam of reporters wanting to see the source of the commotion. To our surprise, Richard motioned for Pieta to steer them toward the front porch. He was ready to talk to them.

As Richard stepped onto his porch, reporters stood in a semi-circle around him, microphones tilted in Richard's direction. Richard bowed his head and began to speak very softly. The crowd and reporters began to whisper.

"Be quiet. Be quiet," members of the crowd murmured. "He's going to say something."

"It seems," he said softly, "we have discovered a story that begged to be told thirty-six hundred years ago...."

Pieta and I looked at each other and knew in that moment that we were witnessing a quantum shift in the world.

The Astonishing Dream of JOB

10

Spiritual Truths

91. In the beginning we believe in the heart but do not know it.

92. Our narcissism implies we do not need self-love; we need control.

93. Those who KNOW are restored; those who fake this character are slaves to the ego.

94. Control is built into the human condition because we know what we are capable of.

95. The ego is our conscience UNTIL we become conscious.

96. The human shadow is an ego asleep, not evil.

97. Message in an emotional storm: Why we suffer? Be—Cause!

98. To BE our true self CAUSES an effect in the world.

99. We cannot believe the ego until we know it.

100. Mercy: is setting the self free for time serving the ego.

The Astonishing Dream of JOB

Epilogue

Anyone waiting to see Pieta at his home office would find a general mess of files leaning against the wall. There is a strong dusty old book smell permeating the air. Splattered on the walls are framed photographs of Pieta with well-known scholars, newspaper clippings about his mentor Richard, and photographs of the broken pottery.

There is an old newspaper clipping of a young, skinny kid reported to have graduated ahead of his classmates. The article is about Pieta entering college. Other wrinkled papers appear to be hieroglyphs, codex interpretations, formulas, theories, various hypotheses, and recent clippings about the community's reaction to the dream text. Many of the documents have Arabic writing, broken wax seals, and dated gold and bright red passport stamps with round symbols in the bottom corners—among them evidence of our journey two years ago.

"Job's experience as a dream is analogous to an ancient wisdom teaching," the paper said. "It represents a spiritual awakening and a dramatic attempt to explore the perennial problem of human suffering." Some papers even reported that the cathartic and imaginative transformation of the Job figure was literally and intellectually comparable to Shakespeare's treatment of Hamlet or Goethe's use of Faust.

I haven't seen Pieta in the two years since we went public with the dream text. Today, we are nestled in his cluttered office, expounding on a recent article in USA Today. "More

The Astonishing Dream of JOB

Americans are tailoring religion to fit their needs," he tells me. "And religion statistics expert George Barna says, with a wry hint of exaggeration, that America is headed for 310 million people with 310 million religions."

In his sphere of academia, Pieta, my respected mentor and friend, is struggling to understand what it takes to hold the public's attention. He sits restlessly at his desk striving to grasp what they missed. A creature of compassion and observer of the human condition, he is a prisoner of the events of the last two years.

"Has our devotion been in vain my old friend?" Pieta asks frustrated.

There is a prideful side to Pieta and a strong sense of social responsibility. He is not simply just an intellectual.

"It is ironic in human learning that one has to align with the dark to escape the consequences of truth," I answer. "Not in vain, but maybe still not in people's awareness."

"How is that possible?" he continues. "Most would agree that a shift in consciousness is imminent in our culture and that integrity and a demand for accountability is at an all-time high. The cathartic message of Job is huge. Meanwhile, nothing….nothing! Is the influence of the conservative and religious right really that powerful?"

Pieta is not devoted to learning for its own sake. This has always been what I've most respected about him. He pursues knowledge with the intent to improve and understand the plight of what it means to be human. This is an important part of his character. His frustration breaks the surface rarely, but in this case it is quite visible.

"Insight," I answer. "For a spontaneous revelation to fully take hold, it must teach people about the fundamental truths of life. If it does not do this, they will likely reject it. With the aid of this dream text, we were able to step outside

Epilogue

the theological understanding of suffering, as it alone has been insufficient. It is surprising that people won't embrace knowledge that is based upon a real inner experience!"

"Yes, yes," he says. "Experience trumps what cannot be understood cognitively. Certainly, we are more than our dogma. All of the media coverage and press about understanding the universe and consciousness and we miss the opportunity to understand the inner workings of a man who predates Christ!"

"Maybe the public views short cuts to the truth, especially if they're metaphysical, as vain," I reply.

Pieta seems only partially aware of my comment.

"Yes, but..." he continues. "To understand the universe is to understand man's inner nature. It's such classic ego to be so fascinated by the external so we can avoid the responsibility for what is going on inside of us."

Pieta turns the translated pages of Job's dream, coming upon the portion of the interpretation that redefines compassion as suffering with another human being versus suffering for them. The mere realization that self-directed compassion is, in fact, self-love fills Pieta with some satisfaction. For a moment, his restless despondency is quiet and relieved.

"I feel such a resonance with this message, don't you?" he asks. "The amount of literature and research that goes into the discussion of our emotional health, self-worth, self-esteem, and here the public is ignoring an explanation of why self-love eludes so many."

"Yes, my friend. It resonates with me too," I answer. "But there is a definite gulf in our culture between the ego's perspective and the heart's truth. It's hard to imagine, but maybe people think to possess both is impossible."

The Astonishing Dream of JOB

Pieta needs my support. The non-reaction by the mainstream public to the new messages of Job is shattering to him. Pieta, who rarely identifies himself with the culture, shrinks in dismay. What he sees in the Job message is in accord with his ideas of the human condition. Job's unplanned insight saved his life—even in the face of his internal and irrational opposition. Real change—change that matters—rarely comes from passive submission to life's problems. No matter how such insights come about, they benefit everyone when they are shared.

"Job's catharsis represents so much," he continues. "Change and movement, harmony and conflict, death and rebirth, all are exactly in line with the world's greatest spiritual teachings."

I think to myself how barren my learning would be if not for my proximity to Pieta's urge to grasp the meaning of life. He has always applied himself without a sense of limitations. I have truly been his pupil. Following him around the world, without always knowing why, my imagination has paled in comparison to his, and yet we complement each other. Modesty and a loyal deference to him as mentor and friend, combined with my steadfastness, has been a good combination.

"The value of subjective emotion is underestimated in this new consciousness," I say. "It comes from the heart, and is an outpouring of the physical side of our being."

"Yes, and what matters most is our attitude about the world in which we live," he replies. "This attitude is the experience within our soul, where fundamentalism has no place."

"I agree," I say. "The truths of religion are not revealed by history, archaeology, or even the church. Job knew this because of his heart."

Epilogue

"How far have we really come?" Pieta asks. "History is always interpreted subjectively and the facts are then adjusted to support someone else's agenda. The literalists and historians are powerless when it comes to approaching the truth. Sadly, by repeating history today, we as a people are making a shocking commentary about the state of our mind—confused."

"Yes," I agree. "Not much of a shift in consciousness, is it? Job's experience as a dream is subjective but pure. There is great wisdom in his emotional journey to awaken. It is society's loss to not see this!"

Pieta, tired from our discussion, decides he needs to rest. He's found little relief in our observations, and I'm used to him needing to retreat and have space to himself. I am staying through dinner, so I plan to use the time to read. "Enlightenment, if nothing else," he remarks as he closes the door, "...is supposed to come with some certainty!"

Sitting in his office alone, I am haunted by a feeling of smallness. Here we are, two experts in human adversity, both seekers of the secrets of the universe, and each of us is equally dumbfounded. I reflect on how close we came to an eternal and human truth about compassion. If self-love that arises out of suffering and contemplation can lift others above the limitations of disability and trauma, imagine what this same gentleness can do for the planet.

The message of Job's dream comes with a supreme stroke of irony; it is founded upon the concept of man's nature. The tragedy, if we are honest with ourselves, is universal. It's not merely that we have inadequate knowledge, or a distorted idea of compassion, or even the lack of human experience. Rather, it is all of these. Alongside the eternal forces of the universe, man is tiny. In spite of our declaration of consciousness and oneness with all that is.

The Astonishing Dream of JOB

What is left for us? Can we continue along the same lines as before? Are we still limited by the conditioning of thousands of years, or can we treat ourselves more favorably with what we now know from Job's catharsis—and make a quantum leap ahead?

Foot Notes

[1] *Oswald J. Chambers (born July 24, 1874, in Aberdeen, Scotland; died November 15, 1917 in Egypt) was a prominent early twentieth-century Protestant Christian minister and teacher, best known as the author of the widely-read devotional My Utmost for His Highest.*

[2] *What The (Bleep) Do We Know? 2004 20th Century Fox, Directed and Written by: Betsy Chasse, Mark Vicente, and William Arntz.*

[3] *Emoto, Masura: The Hidden Messages in Water, Atria Books, September 20, 2005.*

About the Author

Ernie Vecchio is also the author of The Soul's Intent and Big Tail – Small Kite, as well as the founder of the Institute for Compassionate Living. In his extensive career as a trauma psychologist he discovered that when ego or personality was stripped away, his patients had a unique opportunity to recover a truer and authentic self. In most cases, he observed them establish a relationship with soul, spirit, and ego that were aligned with their heart's desire. He calls this process mediating within or finding one's place of compromise. The result was a more meaningful life and choices that were purposeful and goal-oriented. In his twenty-five+ years of working with severe trauma patients, he developed a psychospiritual understanding of that which divides us all: self-judgment. Those willing to explore and heal this division internally discover a broader and more compassionate view of the self. The result was forgiveness and a personal freedom to simply BE. He practices in West Virginia and consults nationally and internationally.

www.theinstituteforcompassionateliving.com

www.ingramcontent.com/pod-product-compliance
Lightning Source LLC
Chambersburg PA
CBHW071452040426
42444CB00008B/1313